Ghosts of the North Coast

Legends, Mysteries and Haunted Places of the North Coast

Doug Dziama
and
Jennifer Dziama Teed

Second Chance Publications
Gettysburg, PA 17325

Copyright © 2013 Doug Dziama and Jennifer Dziama Teed

Published by   Second Chance Publications
P.O. Box 3126
Gettysburg, PA. 17325

WARNING! The stories herein are fully protected by U. S. Federal copyright laws. Unauthorized copying, reproduction, recording, broadcasting, derivative works and public performance, by any individual or company without written consent of the publisher and author are strictly prohibited. Federal copyright laws will be vigorously enforced and infringements will be prosecuted to the fullest extent of the law, which can include damages and lawyers' fees to be paid by the infringer of copyright.

ISBN 10: 0-9849063-9-8
ISBN 13: 978-0-9849063-9-0

Photos by authors or are public domain unless otherwise credited. Original cover design by Carol Nesbitt

*To Sahana, Charlie, and Megan,
our own little Ghosts & Goblins*

Table of Contents

Acknowledgements 6

Introduction 9

Death On The Pacific Express 11

The Perpetual Spirit 21

The Cryptic Fort 27

Of Wine And Other Spirits 35

The Timeless Arcade 43

The Curse Of The Painted Pony 51

Where Have All The Children Gone 59

Shine On Crescent Moon 65

The Spectral Handmaiden 71

Depart All Ye Stranded Souls 79

Lake Erie Monster: Creature Or Myth 87

Stars And Stripes By The Bay 95

Endnotes 101

About The Authors 103

Acknowledgements

This work is actually the sum total of bits and pieces from persons willing to share their experiences and tell us their stories. It was also made possible by the support we received from industry professionals who encouraged us to go forward with this work. And finally, this book could not have come to fruition without the support of family members and friends who assisted in research, photo shoots, and even babysitting.

We would first like to thank Karlene Dziama and Joe Teed who devoted their time and offered their support. Also to Sue Dziama who accompanied us to Cedar Point to "capture" images of the mysterious Mueller wooden horses. Special thanks to Jerry and Lois Teed, who donated their time watching the little ones, and to Sarah Ooms, Penny Kaz, Kathleen Whelan, Sophia Hewitt, Eliza Marroni, Nicol Albanese, and Kristin Porubsky for their help and encouragement.

On a professional level, we would like to thank Mark Nesbitt, author of the *Ghosts of Gettysburg* book series, who included a paranormal experience that our family witnessed in his book, *Ghosts of Gettysburg IV*, inspiring us to write ghost stories of our own. He encouraged us on more than one occasion to do this work. And to his wife Carol, who spent a night with Mark at Captain Montague's B&B and shared her experience.

As for the stories themselves, there are numerous contributors that deserve mention. Many thanks to Keith Jenkins, President of the Westlake Historical Society for his help with the Clague Playhouse story, and to Dick Parker, the head librarian at the Clague Museum. The following actors and stage hands contributed information as well: Greg Dziama, Mary Stoie, Charlotte Crews, Barb Brown, Russ Kilpatrick, Al Archambault, and George Theiss, President of the Clague Players.

Special thanks to our Aunt Marge Dziama, who at age seven (she is now 95 years old) witnessed her dad, Father Wasily, put on vestments to exorcise an unwelcome spirit from a nearby residence. The story she had to tell was nothing short of remarkable. Additional thanks to Rev. Father Basil Stoyka, pastor of S.S. Peter & Paul Orthodox Church, for sharing his extraordinary experiences with us.

The Arcade Building story had many contributors who we would like to recognize as well. Thanks to President Rodney Beals of the Black River Historical Society and to Jon Veard, developer of the Renovated Arcade Building, for granting us interviews. We would also like to thank Paulette Kerpics and Steve Kerpics, residents at the Arcade, and Rene' Dore, who bore witness to the Arcade the night it burned.

Many thanks to Judy Tann, Innkeeper at Captain Montague's Bed-and-Breakfast for allowing us to tour her home and for telling us her story. Additional thanks go to Meg and Larry Gassert of the Hamilton County Fire Department for their input after spending numerous nights at Captain Montague's.

At the Mon Ami Restaurant and Winery, we received great information from their employees. A special thanks to Manager Julie Mathis for her apparition photo, and to Dave Rose, Debbie Griffin, Winemaker Archie Stinson, Debbie Brough, and Mary Ann McKee for their contributions.

Our trip to Fort Meigs was enhanced by Rebecca Scott's article for the *Toledo Blade* about the ghost walks, which included an interview with us. Special thanks to Dan Woodard (staff at Fort Meigs), Lisa Leibfacher (Ohio Historical Society), and the reenactors who gave us a tour of the fort.

The following Cedar Point employees were extremely helpful and need to be mentioned: Captain Ed Ellis, historian at the park and paddlewheel captain; Janice Witherow of Public Relations; Vickie Vandenbout, Susan Shickley, Marge Swenson, Ed Kaman, and Mike and Barb Herdus.

Special thanks to Tom Solberg, owner of the Huron Lagoons Marina, for his testimonials from area fisherman of "monster" sightings on Lake Erie. Tom offered a "bounty" and constructed a live holding area for anyone who captured the notorious beast. We would also like to thank Carrie Sowden, Archeological Director of the Great Lake Historical Society for offering her scientific input.

Thanks to Margaret Lance Chaney from the Ohio Genealogical Society for her help with the Swift's Hollow/Gore Orphanage piece, and to Dawn Rangel for her son's chilling story.

We would also like to thank the Ashtabula Chamber of Commerce for their help in the train disaster story, and the Rev. Virgil Reeve of the 1st Baptist Church in Ashtabula for his phone interview on the subject.

A special thank you goes to Bret Klun, Manager of the Crescent Tavern, who gave us a behind the scenes tour of the building, and to Maggie Beckford and Susie Cooper of the Lake Erie Historical Society for their input.

On a professional level, Doug would like to thank Rick Fisher, founder and Administrator of the Paranormal Society of Pennsylvania. Rick contracted Doug as regular contributor in his publication, *Paranormal Pennsylvania and Beyond*, where a version of ten of the eleven stories in *Ghosts of the North Coast* were previously published.

Introduction

When we first asked Mark Nesbitt, author of the *Ghosts of Gettysburg* book series, to describe his work, he cleverly referred to it as "faction." His work marries historically recognized factual information with theories, or speculation that are drawn by him along with others who gave eyewitness accounts or professional opinions based on field expertise. Not only were we inspired by Mr. Nesbitt's writing, we became inspired by his style of "faction". We believe that "faction" should become a new section in every bookstore and library across the country. We are proud to offer *Ghosts of the North Coast* as our contribution to this unique genre.

We would categorize ghosts as "faction." No one can say for sure that ghosts exist. However, if you ask every eyewitness to a paranormal event, they will swear that their experience was real. In that place and time they saw, heard, or even in some cases, felt something that they could not quite process. We know that first hand, for we were eyewitnesses to our own ghostly encounter.

We were on a covered bridge in Gettysburg, Pennsylvania, after a long hot day of visiting the historic Civil War battlefields. Much to our surprise, we saw something downright uncanny and eerie. To this day we don't know exactly what we saw, but we are convinced beyond a reasonable doubt that what we saw

Introduction

was indeed something paranormal. As Mr. Nesbitt appropriately titled our story in *Ghosts of Gettysburg IV*, it certainly was "A Bridge to Nowhere." The person/figure/being that we saw was at the end of the bridge in a manual wheelchair with his head hanging to the side. There was absolutely no evidence of how he could have gotten there. There was no entrance to that end of the bridge, merely a dirt pathway. Even a motorized wheelchair would have had difficulty. We collectively described it as a lifeless body that appeared to be made of straw rather than flesh and that, accompanied by a strange feeling, told each of us that something was off. None of us walked to the opposite end of the bridge to investigate. You could call it chickening out, and a lifeless man in a wheelchair is hardly threatening, but we were afraid that we were right. Walking to the end of the bridge might have verified our suspicions. We were definitely not ready for that.

Even if you have never had an experience of the unknown, you may be open to the possibility that there are spirits who are still attached to this world for some reason. Maybe there is something that they need to resolve before moving to the afterlife. Who knows, maybe there will eventually be enough tangible evidence to support what many of us already believe in our minds and hearts.

Though we've seen these scenarios countless times in horror movies, there is nothing more frightening than a real-life ghost story. We have offered our explanations for each of these ghostly encounters, but we invite you to draw your own conclusions and get ready to have some fun.

Cheers and Happy Hauntings,

Doug Dziama
Jennifer Dziama Teed

Death On The Pacific Express

*Lora, Lora, still we love thee,
Tho' we see thy form no more,
And we know thou'll come to meet us
When we reach the mystic shore.*

—Philip P. Bliss
From his song *Lora Vale*

Dr. Stephen Smith held the fragile skull with both hands as he made some perplexing observations. He had received a court order to examine the remains of Charles Collins, former Chief Engineer of the Lake Shore & Michigan Southern Railroad. The victim had been found shot to death at his Cleveland residence on January 20, 1877, a few weeks after the Ashtabula Train Disaster. Collins' post-traumatic depression, it was said, was to blame for the self-inflicted gunshot wound through his mouth.

He glanced at the clock and recorded the date, April 26, 1878, as he held the brittle brain case in one hand. Approximately fifteen and one half months had elapsed since the bridge collapsed into the gorge. He probed into the large irregular opening behind the left ear, approximately two-and-one-half by one and a half inches in size. Its precise edges defied original speculation that this was the exit wound, which would have been jagged and fragmented. Also, the absence of powder stains indicated the barrel's end was no less than four inches from the head. He concluded that the projectile entered through the head and not the mouth.

Mr. Collins' blood-soaked body was discovered, he was told, in a very natural position in his own bed with his next-day's wardrobe lying neatly on a chair. His left arm lay at his side still clutching the half-empty military revolver (which he owned). Dr. Smith suddenly recalled that the victim was right-handed.

"If that were so," he thought to himself, "the victim would have had to hyperextend his left arm behind him and discharge the weapon with his non-dominant hand. Furthermore, the violent recoil would have propelled the gun away from him." He recorded the time once again before submitting his concluding statement: "my opinion is that Mr. Collins came to his death by a shot wound inflicted by other hands than his own.[1]

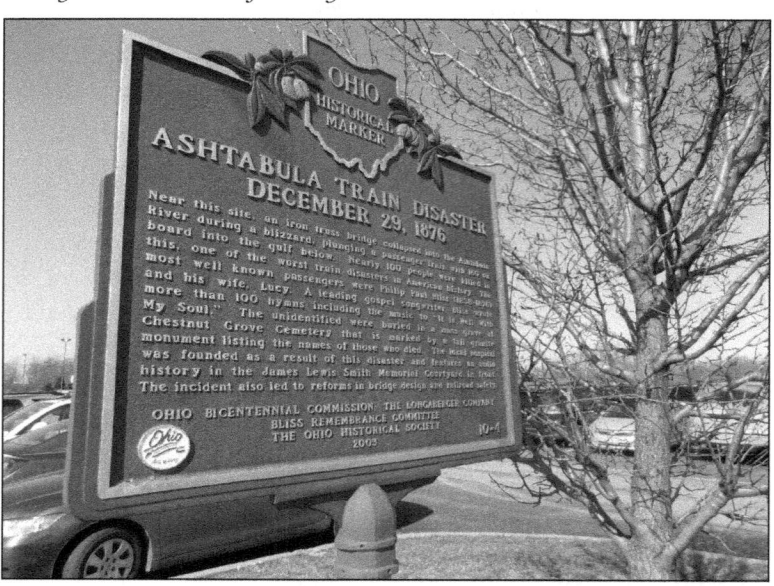

Ohio Historical Marker at the Ashtabula Train Disaster site.

It still goes down as one of the worst train wrecks in American history and one of Ohio's biggest unsolved mysteries. The mystery to which we are referring is the death of Charles Collins, chief engineer of Lake Shore & Michigan Southern Railroad. Was it guilt due to the unnecessary loss of innocent lives that motivated him? If so, this guilt would seem too much to bear, and it would be easy and quick to explain his untimely demise on a suicide. That is until an autopsy was performed. Could someone have murdered Collins and tried to cover it up as a suicide? Did someone design the perfect crime scene, which even included a forged suicide letter to his wife? After Dr. Smith's findings, things were not adding up.

Could one man have prevented one of the worst train wrecks from happening? Maybe. If it was murder, who would want Collins dead? A grieving relative of one of the Ashtabula victims? Railroad president Amasa Stone? After all, Collins was found dead the same day that he had appeared before a legislative investigation committee for thorough questioning. Did someone want to permanently stop Collins from exposing the railroad company's cost-saving negligence? And to top it all off, the person who requested the court-ordered exhumation and autopsy was never identified. This is a plot that seems straight out of Hollywood. The facts are stranger than fiction.

The Ashtabula River today is tranquil and shallow as it quietly meanders toward Lake Erie. Only the towering bluffs that parallel its now torpid waters remind us of the power it once possessed. The chasm below remains much as it was on December 29, 1876. Stretching about a half mile from north to south, it plunges to depths of up to one hundred twenty-five feet and has been dubbed, "the gorge" or "the gulf."

Railroads have been an important part of American history for over 200 years. The railroad system has not only provided transportation of goods and passengers, but it has employed many Americans. In the 1830s-1850s railway building was booming. The industry continued to be our nation's primary mode of transportation until the 1920s and 1930s, when automobiles and airplanes were introduced. Along with the Great Depression, all of these factors contributed to the decline of railroad usage. When the industry was booming, Charles Collins was a widely respected railroad employee with over 30 years in the industry.

When the Lake Shore & Michigan Southern Railroad decided to build a new Howe-type iron truss bridge over the valley's 152-foot span, it met with outspoken skepticism, especially from Charles Collins who called it "experimental" at best. He quarreled bitterly with railroad President Amasa Stone, who insisted the design was safe and ordered it to be built anyway.

Midway through the project, chief construction engineer Joseph Tomlinson resigned after arguing with President Stone that the main braces were in fact too small, having been downsized from the original design. Charles Collins agreed, but unlike Tomlinson, remained loyal to the firm. It became disturbingly clear to both men that President Stone's budget and timetable took priority over safety.

The bridge was completed near schedule and was in service for approximately ten years without incident. It loomed menacingly over the hollow. The twin tracks ran over a linear linkage of braces, beams, and bolts that were most abundant at the middle, giving it a sagging or "bellied" appearance. Those who stopped found the image disturbing.

The railway hugged the Lake Erie shoreline through Western Pennsylvania, Ashtabula County, Ohio, and destinations west. This is the infamous "Snow Belt" area over which cruel northwest winds howl across half-frozen lake water, churning up enormous flakes of wet, heavy snow. Temperatures commonly plunge to the teens with sub-zero wind chills and near-blizzard conditions. Snow accumulations often exceed twenty inches in only a few hours.

The region was pelted with such a storm on Friday, December 29, 1876, when the Pacific Express No. 5 steamed into Erie, Pennsylvania, to pick up additional passengers. The train consisted of eleven cars that were towed by two locomotives: the front-running "Socrates," engineered by Dan McGuire from Erie; followed by "Columbia" with Gustavus "Pap" Folsom from Cleveland at the controls. Both men were highly qualified and experienced operators.

Of the estimated 160 passengers on board, none was more renowned than Philip P. Bliss, a leading gospel songwriter. Born in 1838, Bliss and his wife Lucy resided in Rome, Pennsylvania, where he studied music and composed such beloved hymns as "Hold the Fort" and "Hallelujah, What a Savior!" The couple was travelling to Chicago to attend a religious revival.

At 3:00 P.M. the ill-fated train rolled out of Erie bound for Ashtabula and a 5:15 arrival straight into the teeth of the monstrous "Clipper," a Canadian low-pressure system. The ferocious winds increased as evening advanced, with a darkness that would obscure even the most merciful and loving God. Engineer Folsom described it as "the worst storm I have ever experienced!"

The relentless wind and snow would not allow the train to stay on schedule. At about ten minutes before 7:00, the Pacific Express passed through Conneaut, Ohio, which lies approximately thirteen miles east of Ashtabula. At 7:27 the No. 5 rounded a curve at the gulf's eastern edge, providing engineer McGuire with a visual of the snow-covered bridge and the depot lights beyond.

Watching vigilantly from the other side was telegraph operator William Ansell, anxious about the overdue train. He looked away for an instant and then looked back to observe Socrates' headlight as it came through the turn and approached the bridge. His eyewitness testimony, as told to the Ashtabula Sentinel, would chill the blood of even the most callous heart.

"I was startled by a crash and looking around was horrified at seeing the lights of the coaches disappearing down the gulch into the creek under the bridge. My first impression was that the engine had jumped the track, gone over the bridge, and was pulling the coaches after it. I had friends on board and feeling what must be their awful fate I stood spellbound, terrified beyond measure and absolutely unable to move."

Engineer Dan McGuire stated that Socrates had just completed the crossing when he felt a violent jar and a strain on his rear coupling that pulled the locomotive back toward the edge. He opened the throttle and regained his forward motion just in time to save the lead engine. The second engine and remaining cars plummeted with the buckling bridge into the river below.

According to the Ashtabula Sentinel, "a few minutes after the crash the flames burst simultaneously from nearly every car. A gentleman, who was first at the scene, says he saw a young and finely dressed girl of about ten years of age struggling in vain to release her hips from the weight which was crushing her slender form, and close behind her were the flames, which in another instant enwrapped her in their embrace. Here was a fine-appearing gentleman, of middle age, sitting bolt upright in his seat and unable to extricate himself, calmly awaiting the flames, which soon claimed their victim. There were bodies floating out from the wreck. A crowd soon made their way to the burning debris, and, with the aid of axes and ropes, many were extricated, placed on stretchers, and taken to the top of the hill."

Witnesses said that Charles Collins himself was there, standing in waist-deep water assisting persons from the wreckage. At the time when the dead and injured were being transported, a mob mentality developed from the lack of law and order. Looters plundered money and other valuables that were strewn among twisted metal and human wreckage. Precious jewelry was wrestled from injured and lifeless bodies, and even more despicable, from pieces of mutilated or burnt flesh, forever stripping the victim's identity and denying closure to the next of kin.

Search and rescue continued through the night and for the next few weeks. Pieces of bone and flesh found floating below the wreckage were taken to the freight house and placed in boxes with a white numbered placard and labeled "unidentifiable." When recovery efforts finally ceased, it was estimated that seventy-one persons survived with ninety-nine dead or missing. Both engineers lived, despite Columbia's crash into the ravine.

Charles Collins had been observed weeping bitterly at his wife's parents' Ashtabula residence days after the crash, believing that those who had trusted him had now turned against him. He tendered his resignation to the railroad and it was immediately rejected.

On Monday, January 15, not wanting to be alone, he asked his assistant, Mr. I. C. Brewer, to stay at his Cleveland home. Mrs. Collins had already left for Ashtabula to attend Friday's Memorial Service for the crash victims and to stay with her parents. On Wednesday morning Collins faced intense questioning about the tragedy from the newly assembled Legislative Investigation Committee. When Mr. Brewer did not see him at the office that day, he assumed Collins had gone to Ashtabula and did not stay the night. On Friday, when Collins was still unaccounted for, Brewer sent a telegraph to all points without a reply. He returned to the Collins' home on Saturday and questioned the servants who said they had not seen him. Still not satisfied, he searched the house and found the blood-spattered bedroom.

Main Avenue in downtown Ashtabula is still a tidy row of mercantile shops that has maintained a simple yet eclectic charm. There is little evidence of the horror that occurred here over a century ago. Only Collins Boulevard, a historical marker near the hospital, and the patina coated bell at the fire station that tolled relentlessly that night, remain. Even some citizens are unaware of this catastrophic event. When I asked directions to the railroad viaduct, a hospital orderly responded, "which one?"

But in the minds of many, the legend lives on. Some say that the spirits of the accident victims return to the bottom of the bridge every December 29th. After visiting the area, it is not somewhere we want to return to anytime soon, especially at night. Except for an occasional trickle from a small eddy, the silence is deafening. We wondered what secrets the water had not yet given up: a rusty old rail, or perhaps a piece of heirloom jewelry? Only the river knows for sure.

We proceeded down Main Avenue to Grove Drive, turned, and drove up the high bluff that is Chestnut Grove Cemetery. The crypt of Charles Collins looms atop the summit, shrouded in a grayish mist. Some say that wailing sounds, like that of a banshee, are emitted from deep within its stone walls. We could not help but notice a fresh flower had been placed in a link of the chain that secured the iron gated entrance.

Crypt of Charles Collins at Chestnut Grove Cemetery in Ashtabula.

On May 30, 1895, an elegant monument was unveiled with the names of twenty-six "Unrecognizable Dead" etched at its base. Local legend says that men in long coats with watch fobs and top hats, and women wearing lengthy dresses and veils, are seen gathering around the granite marker. Among those listed, Mr. & Mrs. P. P. Bliss. As I meditated for a moment, I could almost hear his dirge to Lora Vale, only this time in a joyous arrangement.

Monument marking the final resting place of the unidentified remains.

    Impending death often carries a vision. Some see a figure clothed in white waiting for them at the end of a tunnel. Quite possibly, Philip P. Bliss had a similar vision when the bridge gave way: that of the sweet innocence that was Lora Vale as she ran to greet him on the banks of the "mystic shore."

The Perpetual Spirit

...for a spirit hath not flesh and bones, as you and me have
—Luke 24:39

Imagine attending a production at your community theatre company and some time between the first and second acts you notice a hologram-like figure in the lighting booth. The figure looks human, but your gut tells you that it is something else. Now imagine being an actor in this performance, observing the spiritual interruption from the stage. For the actors and audience this is business as usual at the Clague Playhouse.

Although he was a decent hard-working man, Walter Clague maintained a somewhat ghastly appearance. His receding hairline exposed an oversized head that was surrounded by tufts of disheveled, white hair. A drooping beard failed to minimize his protruding chin, drawing even more attention to a narrow crooked nose. His sunken piercing eyes could, if you let them, penetrate the depths of your very soul. Someone once remarked that old Walter looked like he could haunt a house or just about anything for that matter.

The son of an immigrant farmer, Walter was born in 1846. He and his eight siblings were raised on a seventy-eight acre fruit farm in rural Cuyahoga County, Ohio. As was customary for that time, his father taught farming to each of his nine children, with young Walter rising to the top of his trade.

He had an interest in collecting gadgets, which resulted in his acquiring the first farming implements in the region. He was also the first to grow tobacco and he developed the area's first gas well. It was this innovative spirit that placed him at the pinnacle of a developing society, allowing the family to become very well off.

Some of his brothers and sisters had an aptitude for wise investments, especially his sister Sophronia, who became the family spendthrift. Even though they acquired a good deal of wealth, the family was tightly bound together and became quite philanthropic, always willing to loan money to those less fortunate.

Walter and Sophronia inherited the family property where they spent their working lives. When they retired, Walter donated the farm to the village, but with two stipulations: the land was to be used as a park and Walter and his sister be allowed to live out their earthly existence there. Walter died in 1934.

Walter's desire was to preserve the farm's original appearance and the ground that had been toiled on by his family. The village accepted his generous offer of seventy-eight acres, agreeing to develop them into a memorial park.

Walter's dream was shattered in 1967 when the village leased his beloved barn to a local theatre group. In November of that year, the group presented the show, *Sunday in New York* in front of a packed house that included a number of local dignitaries. This inaugural performance kicked off a number of successful seasons in the intimate theatre, which seated only 85 persons.

Legend has it that this acquisition made Walter very angry. Because he was not a mean-spirited individual, he chose to manifest his anger in a mischievous and somewhat playful fashion. He began showing up at rehearsals and shows, and developed a distinction for himself with the group's players, stagehands and technicians. He even disrupted a building renovation in September 1996.

*Walter and Sophronia Clague.
Photo courtesy of the Clague Museum.*

"It was a strange, dark September night," recalled a former theatre president. "I was doing remodeling in one of the restrooms. I took the door off the hinges and placed my toolbox just outside the hall to my left. I was sitting on the floor, Indian-style, working on the sink. I was using a trouble light and a flashlight. Suddenly, I bumped the trouble-light I was using and it went out, and when I reached for my flashlight, it wasn't there. My toolbox was gone, too. Both were found about three feet away down the hall, with the flashlight standing on end. I continued to work, but yelled 'OK, Walt, I've got to get this done.' I had no more trouble after that."

A lighting and sound technician offers another strange testimonial. "During the performance of *If It's Monday, This Must Be Murder* (Dec. 1999), one of the persons in the booth felt something brush against his leg, but when he turned around, no one was there. An audience member later remarked that she saw Walter lurking in the booth at that precise moment."

She also said that a music box used on some of the sets would mysteriously go on and off by itself. "I utilized it in one of the shows recently and all of a sudden it just stopped playing. Within a few moments it started playing again."

Walter surprised one of the set designers, as well, who testified that he was painting the stage floor when a coffee can with nuts and bolts fell over. He pushed the can back out of the way. It fell again, this time flying across the room.

And, of course, the actors have had their run-ins with Old Walter. One of them explained that in 1996 they were rehearsing for the show *Company*, when a coffee pot that was a stage prop suddenly turned on. No one knew who did it, not even the stage manager. Although no one saw him, they concluded that Walter must have been responsible.

Actors and long time members of the Clague Playhouse group have learned to take Walter in stride and embrace the haunting of their beloved stage. They even do fundraisers around Halloween. The actors dress up as members of the Clague family. They pose for family pictures and reenact some of the hauntings that have taken place in the building. To us it would seem like poking the hornets nest—a sure fire way to stir up more hauntings. This would normally be terrifying if in fact Walter's ghost was not the benign, playful character that witnesses say he is.

Though we speculate that spirits cling to their mortal existence due to unfinished business, suppose the unfinished business is a dream that never came to be? Maybe an aspiration that did not materialize in their earthly lives becomes the sole purpose of their ghostly afterlives.

Though the *Sun Herald* maintained that the mortal Clagues were "boring," Walter's spiritual alter ego seems anything but. Many believe that Walter's paranormal horseplay is due to his disapproval of his beloved farm being turned into a theatre. But, what if he had dreams of his own that went unfulfilled? Maybe he would liked to have been on the very stage that he perpetually haunts.

If Walter had aspired to be an actor, he would definitely have been more sitcom than Shakespeare. Picture a supporting character, after witnessing one of Walter's vintage practical jokes, hands on her hips, shaking her head in false disapproval, saying "That Walter." The canned audience laughter would be cued and you would have a comedy reminiscent of the quintessential 1980s sitcom.

Clague Playhouse in Westlake, Ohio.

Yes, it's true that the barn became a theatre against his stated wishes, but let us not pity poor Walter too much. His farm did become a municipal park in beautiful Westlake, Ohio[1], and the playhouse, which is currently in its 85th season, continues to bear his name. And, Walter was permitted to live on his beloved homestead until his death, and allegedly remains there to this very day.

Walter's presence at the Clague Playhouse, is almost as necessary as it is expected, for he appears to be devising his own unique marketing plan from beyond the grave.

If you are in the area and wish to take in a production at the Playhouse, don't be surprised if your ticket buys you two shows for the price of one.

The Cryptic Fort

Follow me, and let the dead bury their dead."

—Matthew 8:22

He rested his weary eyes, casting a blank stare into the night. The advancing darkness ushered in a howling wind and icy drizzle that had chilled him to the bone.

The embattled bastion, made of earthen walls and traverses, was shrouded in an eerie mist that resembled a foggy English moor. Smoldering campfires produced heavy smoke and crackling embers mimicked an occasional musket shot. The odor of death abounded everywhere, in spite of them.

The cries of the wounded harmonized with the wind, while the dead, having already begun their decomposition process, awaited the harvest. Feeling tired and nauseous, Private Alfred M. Lorrain of the Petersburg (Virginia) Volunteers fixated on the grotesque group that lay at his feet.[1]

The story of Fort Meigs is a bit different from the rest in our collection. For one thing, we can guess the motives for the spirits that haunt it. As we have learned from Gettysburg, it is no mystery that battlegrounds are hotbeds of paranormal activity. It seems logical that there would be unsettled souls in

Fort Meigs given the horror that occurred nearly two hundred years ago. The Fort is literally a collective grave that holds what is left of the war along with the many brave souls who perished and whose life stories will never be told. The violence that took place there was unimaginable not to mention unthinkable. Even filmmakers Quentin Tarantino (*Kill Bill, Jango Unchained*) and Eli Roth (*Hostel, Cabin Fever*), who are known for their excessive gore, would have trouble replicating the battle's horror on-screen.

There is no doubt that war is a version of hell on earth. Through researching our stories, history reminds us that many of the deaths that occurred were unnecessary, the result of a lack of medical advancements. Sadly many died grisly deaths alone and without even a proper burial. This was far too common in the War of 1812, and in Ohio, we have a reminder of lives lost in this bloody war on the battleground of Fort Meigs. We prefer to think of Fort Meigs as a shrine in memory of those who gave their lives, as opposed to the destructive battleground that it once was. We should not forget or dismiss these tragic events in our country's history.

If you are anything like us, you skimmed over the chapter on the War of 1812 in your high school history book. We feel guilty for not remembering what it was even about. Ironically, it is often referred to as "America's Forgotten War" and we've done a great job of forgetting. As a quick refresher, the War of 1812 was a thirty-two month ordeal between the United States, the British Empire and Britain's Indian allies. The war was declared by the United States and was not solely about territory, but rather other issues including trade restrictions brought on by Britain's war with France. Many historians believe that the war was inconsequential, and that after three years of fighting, the six thousand American lives lost were in vain. When the war was over the U.S. and Britain agreed upon a treaty that didn't even resolve the issues that began the war.

The first siege of Fort Meigs began May 1st and lasted until May 9, 1813. The fortress had repelled a relentless shelling from British artillery, followed by an assault from British and Canadian troops under the command of General Henry Proctor, and an Indian Confederation led by the legendary Shawnee Warrior, Tecumseh. The salvo was launched against powder magazines within the fort that were fortified by earthly redoubts and timber, preventing crippling explosions and extensive human casualties. General William Henry Harrison, the garrison's commander, wanting to preserve his small supply of ordinance, used his artillery pieces sparingly, and offered whiskey to any soldier who captured an enemy cannonball and launched it back.

Named for Ohio Governor Return Jonathon Meigs, Jr., the fort was built on a high bluff overlooking the Maumee River near Toledo, Ohio, under the auspices of Major General William H. Harrison. Harrison, who would later become the 9th President of the United States, considered it crucial to fortify Ohio's Northwest Corridor from British attack. (In 1840, Harrison returned to Fort Meigs as a presidential candidate to host a rally that included War of 1812 veterans and a crowd of 25,000.)

The bombardment ended on May 4th with the arrival of fresh, mostly raw, recruits of 1200 Kentucky militiamen under the command of General Green Clay. General Harrison placed half of Clay's recruits under Colonel William Dudley to spearhead an attack north of the fort to "spike" (disable) British artillery on the opposite bank of the Maumee. The remaining 400 soldiers, under the command of Clay, were to assault upriver at the fort's southern end to subdue Indian attacks from the west.

Dudley met with initial success, but his unseasoned troops were seduced into an ambush by Shawnee warriors. Only 150 men escaped, with the rest being captured and forced to "run the gauntlet" at nearby Fort Miamis. This was the barbaric execution of unarmed and naked captives that included tomahawking, clubbing, scalping, and shooting. Tecumseh stopped the violence, accusing British commander Proctor of cowardice, but only after the slaughter of 40 American soldiers. Survivors were taken to nearby British gunboats. Among the victims was Colonel Dudley, whose mutilated remains, with the top of his head missing, were interred at Fort Meigs.

The citadel repulsed a second assault in July 1813, sending the retreating British forces to Fort Stephenson in Fremont, Ohio. Here they attacked and faced total annihilation by a swaggering 21-year-old Major named George Croghan and his cannon, "Old Betsy." Wisely, British General Henry Proctor called off the attack. The expulsion of British forces from Ohio, along with Oliver Hazard Perry's victory on Lake Erie, paved the way for an American invasion of Canada.[2]

But to the victors go the spoils. The first siege of Fort Meigs, which began on April 28th and ended May 5th, had been the most sanguinary, producing 77 dead and around 200 wounded.[3]

Collectively hog-tied at the ankles and dragged into unmarked graves, many bodies were mutilated beyond recognition.

And there were various ways to die here. Exploding shells, canister, and one-ounce balls of lead fired from antiquated muskets could kill, sever, and maim. Wounds often festered from lack of antibiotics, causing death to be slow and agonizing. Captured soldiers faced mutilation by the tomahawk, followed by a brutal scalping.

To cope, many assigned to battlefield burials developed a callousness that would haunt them for a lifetime, viewing the poor, lifeless souls as never having been human. Private Lorrain recorded in his diary: "But now, at this lonely hour, while all the army were wrapped in sleep, except a few widely scattered sentinels, I could look down on this ghastly, disfigured group, without even a tremor stealing over my nerves. I found that my heart had become wretchedly hardened by the scenes...."[4]

In short, Fort Meigs had become a crypt to many who fell here. Some remain entombed for an eternity. Others are eternally restless, searching for something denied to them at death. Here are the stories of two such lost souls.

Amos Stoddard was born in Connecticut in 1762. A veteran of the American Revolution, he relocated to Massachusetts to practice law. He eventually became a State Legislator.

In 1798, he entered the army as a Captain of the 2nd Regiment of Artillery and Engineers. He commanded the upper Louisiana Territory. He received a Major's commission in 1807 and became commander of Artillery at Fort Meigs in 1813.

On May 1, 1813, the opening day of the British bombardment of the garrison, Major Stoddard received a superficial leg wound from an exploding shell. Doctors believed, at first, that the wound was not mortal. But tetanus bacteria contaminated his system, causing a serious neurological disease commonly known as lockjaw. He succumbed to the deadly affliction on May 11th. He was interred the next day near Battery One at Fort Meigs.

Grand Battery at Fort Meigs, believed to be one of three burial sites, and final resting place of Major Amos Stoddard.

Major Stoddard's final hours were agonizing. Fever and muscle spasms took control, causing severe convulsions and foaming at the mouth. Pain contorted his face into a hideous expression. He was unable to speak. His closed lips emitted excruciating, almost inhuman sounds.

Given the choice, Major Stoddard would have opted for a soldier's death, one with glory in the heat of battle. He expired, instead, in extreme pain, and some even say, is searching still for that final ball of lead.

Lieutenant Robert Walker, from Pennsylvania, was perhaps even less fortunate. A member of the Fifth Provisional Battalion, he encountered an untimely and freakish ending to his earthly life.

On March 9, 1813, while duck hunting along the river, Lieutenant Walker was captured by savages and taken to nearby Fort Miamis (Miami) where he was tomahawked and scalped.[5] Hours later, his battered body, the top of its head missing, would surface beneath a layer of ice on the frozen Maumee.

British soldiers would later remark about the cruelty of these executions and the disgusting display of the bloodied scalps dangling from poles to dry in the sun.[6] It is interesting to note that even a fallen deer receives a merciful shot to the heart before it is butchered.

For Lieutenant Walker, he received an honorable burial at Fort Meigs, but was denied a dignified death. It is the belief of many that he still prowls the fort and its surrounding grounds searching, perhaps, for another head of hair.

Today, Fort Meigs is completely restored as a War of 1812 battleground. Each year, school children take organized classroom tours of this piece of history owned by the Ohio Historical Society. The Society's goal is to have visitors receive an experience that is historically accurate. There is a cooking class conducted in a kitchen modeled after those in 1812, and a blacksmithing workshop where visitors can witness the lost art of heating and bending metal.

During encampments at the fort, reenactors have reported seeing large blue lights or orbs floating arrogantly around the fort's interior walls. Some of these orbs were even said to transfigure into human form before vanishing into the dark abyss.

One reenactor shared what he had experienced. "We were set up near the Grand Battery when I saw a group of soldiers in full, authentic uniform moving toward us. Believing they were fellow reenactors, I turned to grab my light, only to witness they had disappeared in a matter of seconds."

Another soldier, camped near Blockhouse #3, observed a gun crew of translucent soldiers preparing to discharge an artillery piece. After turning to throw a log on the fire, he looked back to find they had evaporated into the night air, with only the mute cannon remaining. He walked over to inspect the gun, but found no smell of gunpowder or evidence of anyone having been there.

Blockhouse #3 with ectoplasm (spiritual energy) in the lower left corner.

It is also recorded that a Native American burial ground is believed to exist beyond the walls of the fort near the river, not far from the site of the present day visitor's center. Modern soldiers have witnessed the piercing stare of a warrior through a window in Blockhouse #3. The image, it was said, was peering toward the river, beyond the visitor's center.

In 2003, when Fort Meigs was in the process of being restored to its wartime appearance, "Garrison Ghost Walks" were conducted around Halloween. The walks featured storytellers in authentic period costumes sharing tales around a campfire. Visitors heard about the phantom gunfire, blue lights, "filmy" soldiers, and "the Woman and child" who have been seen staring from Blockhouse #3.

Intrigued by the hype, we decided to take the tour. We chose to visit the fort beforehand to take photographs, only to make a chilling discovery. Just inside the inner walls of the fort's northeast corner were the tracks of a huge and powerful hound, belonging possibly to a Great Dane or Mastiff. Each footprint was the size of a man's closed fist. Guided by an acute sense of smell, the creature entered the fort, perhaps drawn by the scent of ancient blood.

Shortly after entering, the giant beast came to an abrupt halt, his footprints reversing themselves in elongated, desperate strides. It appeared the animal had encountered an "image" of something terrifying, something it couldn't relate to, and possibly not of this world.

A few days later, we stared into the twilight waiting for the ghost walks to begin. The fort had assumed an eerie appearance due to smoke and mist, looking much like a foggy English moor.

As our group approached one of the storytellers, a small boy jumped at a "pop" from the crackling fire. Standing near Amos Stoddard's monument, beneath a grove of trees, a strange, moaning sound was heard. Looking up at the rustling leaves, we smiled. It's probably just the wind....

Of Wine And Other Spirits

"And be not drunk with wine, wherein is excess; but be filled with the Spirit;"

—Ephesians 5:18

Though there is only one Napa Valley, Ohio proudly offers its own winery region along its north coast. These wineries illustrate how wine drinking has become a way of life for Midwesterners, as well as those in other parts of the country. There is the Paper Moon Vineyards of Vermilion, Matus Winery and Vermilion Valley in Wakeman (and coincidentally both located on a stretch of the infamous Gore Orphanage Road), Hermes Winery of Sandusky, Quarry Hill Winery of Berlin Heights, D & D Winery of Norwalk, and John Christ of Avon Lake, just to name a few. It is possible to hit several of these wineries in an afternoon, however, make sure to pace yourself as the wine buzz tends to creep up on a person rather suddenly. That's what we've been told anyway, and in no way something we have learned from our own experiences.

Each of these wineries has something different to offer its customers. Some offer winery tours and tastings, while others offer patios or gardens where guests can leisurely sip its grape infused nectar of the gods.

There is another winery that has it's own unique branding. It offers spirits of the paranormal kind to go with its wine and cheese. Located in Port Clinton, this winery is called Mon Ami Winery. Since it is near both the Jet Express and Miller Ferry, Mon Ami is a great place to stop if you are in no hurry to return home after a day or two of Put-in-Bay or Kelleys Island dwelling. Mon Ami features an elegant dining room, a private banquet room, and a cozy fireside chalet. There is also a cocktail lounge known as "Jimmy's Bar," a gift shop, the wine tasting room, and, of course, the wine cellars. And from what we've been told, some very peculiar happenings have taken place over the years at Mon Ami, beginning with the winery's rich historical past.

The wooden steamer had departed Europe over three and one half weeks before and would be arriving in New York in a few, short hours. One passenger slowly scanned the faces of the other 3rd class travelers and could see his own hopes and dreams in their expressions. He vicariously felt their joy, their excitement, and their sadness.

They had been quartered like sardines in the depths of the ship's hull, having to endure deplorable living and sanitary conditions. They were referred to as "steerage" by the other passengers, who considered them only slightly better than the vermin that dwelled in the bilge beneath them.

He pictured his beloved mother waving good-bye as he boarded the train in his native Germany, and how he would never see her again. A tear formed in the corner of his eye, but quickly evaporated with thoughts of the glorious opportunities ahead of him.

America. Land of the free. And, with the recent end of the Civil War, freedom had no boundaries. Religious, educational, and vocational opportunity abounded everywhere. Here, you could make a name for yourself and build a home.

He was bound for the Black Swamp District of Northwest Ohio, a flat, marshy land that was enjoying a recent population boom. Most of the settlers were German immigrants who went in droves to farm the rich, fertile soil that was exposed after the region was drained.

His final destination was Catawba Island, a 600-acre land parcel that was divided from the mainland by West Harbor, a narrow and shallow channel of water. The "island" had been organized into a separate township exclusively for the cultivation of grapes, which thrived in the warm fall climate of Lake Erie's extended growing season.

He took a construction job at workmen's wages for the Catawba Island Wine Company in 1865. He would later meet a beautiful young woman who became the object of his affections, and whose hand he had asked for in marriage. His "American Dream" was becoming a reality.

At the time of its completion in 1872, the new Cawtaba Island Wine Company building had four floors and was one of the area's most exquisite structures. Built of native limestone from a nearby quarry and finished with black walnut from a local grove, it became a most impressive example of Gothic Architecture.

The pressroom was located on the ground floor, while the second floor was used to age sherry. The upper-level cellar, which was a constant 58 degrees, was utilized for aging still wines. The lower cellar level, with its year-round 50-degree environment, was designated for the storage of sparkling wines.

Renamed Mon Ami, which means "you are my friend," the building survived a devastating fire in 1943 that gutted the inside. The solid limestone structure remained intact and the interior was fully restored back to a working winery. It was remodeled in the 1990's to what it is today. It was during these renovations that numerous strange and unexplainable occurrences took place. Many were so frightening, that some employees will not enter certain areas of the building alone, particularly the wine cellars. They are gloomy and ominous-looking with endless rows of giant wooden barrels. The perfect hiding place for something sinister.

Historic Mon Ami Restaurant and Winery.

One of the two banquet managers at Mon Ami recalled a party in the upper wine cellar. "When I descended the staircase to the bottom, I turned toward the light switch and walked slowly to flip it on. About halfway across the room, I did a complete about-face, flew up the staircase, and stopped only after I had exited the building." A funny feeling had overwhelmed her, and to this day, she cannot enter the wine cellars alone.

The gift shop manager recalled a similar frightening experience when touring the upper wine cellar. Following a group of fifteen people, she began hearing a strange *"click, click, click"* sound. Assuming it was someone joining the tour, she turned around and saw no one. The clicking resumed when the tour continued. Asking the guide about the noise, she received a haunting reply of, "yes, it's the ghost," something she had hoped not to hear.

But strange occurrences are not limited to the wine cellars. The Chalet, which is home to casual dining and warm crackling fires, has had its share of unexplained phenomenon. The house manager shared the following story.

"One night I was there alone. As I got ready to leave, I was behind the chalet bar looking out toward the dining area. Sitting on a brass railing was a blue light. I looked behind and then forward again and there was nobody there. It had mysteriously vanished!"

On another occasion, he was alone and closing up for the night. This time, as he approached the exit with key in hand, someone asked, "are you locking the door?" A chill traveled the entire length of his spine. Looking over his shoulder, he saw no one.

The Main Dining Room, which is an elegant "white tablecloth affair," has had its share of unexplained activity. Of particular interest are the strange occurrences surrounding table 249.

With the dubious distinction of being known as "The Table from Hell," table 249 transforms even the most congenial guest into an ill-mannered ingrate. There are written accounts from several different members of the wait staff stating that all who sit at the table undergo a temporary, inexplicable, personality shift. And the staff is not just talking about patrons sending their food back multiple times. Some describe the table's occupants as "hateful," saying incredibly rude, obnoxious, and highly uncalled for words to the wait staff. All of the staff have noticed the guests returning to their normal behavior upon leaving the "wicked" table. There is no doubt that the staff is *not* fighting over who gets to wait on table 249.

Late one October evening in 1998, the office manager at Mon Ami recalled her terrifying experience in the proximity of table 249.

"I would hear the stories, but was skeptical. I began hearing footsteps above the office. My daughter came that evening to join me in a night time 'health walk' through the restaurant. I walked past table 249 and saw the image of a man sitting there. Even after numerous laps around the room, he would not go away."

Her daughter, who was about six feet ahead of her, turned around and said, "Mom, you're going to think I'm nuts, but…"

"I know what you're going to tell me," said Debbie. Her daughter screamed and ran from the building, never to return.

The other banquet manager recalled a strange occurrence in the hallway leading back storage room.

"I was standing on the wooden dance floor, and when I tried to move my right foot, my shoe stuck to the floor as if I had stepped in tar. I looked down to make sure that my shoe was tied, and it was. After pulling my foot once again, it was released from the floor and my co-manager was able to lead me to the storage room." Upon entering the storage room she felt an icy chill.

She went on to say that the lights in the banquet room often come on "softly" by themselves. She would say aloud, "Okay now, that's enough! Turn them off!" The lights would go off as mysteriously as they had come on.

Incidentally, we give her a lot of credit for attempting to communicate with the spirit. Most people (admittedly maybe even us) might have been so spooked that they would have sprinted out the back door. Especially after receiving confirmation that the spirit is indeed there, perhaps even right beside them.

More recently, on September 30, 2002, the night cleaning man came running out of the Main Dining Room from the vicinity of table 249. Someone had "brushed-up" against his arm as he was working. Again, like the others before him, he turned around to see no one.

It would be interesting to find out how these personality-transformed guests tip their waiters. Perhaps Mon Ami should automatically add a 20% gratuity charge to all those who sit at the dreaded table. If you wish to visit Mon Ami and sit at table 249, do not use this legend as an excuse to act like a complete jerk. If the table's permanent paranormal patron temporarily poisons your mind, well....

After several strange instances and to indulge their curiosity, the owners of Mon Ami called in a psychic from Cleveland to try to identify this strange and uninvited visitor. After exploring all of the winery floors, she concluded that the spirit was "your protector here," but offered no further explanation or identification.

Apparition in kitchen at Mon Ami.
Photo courtesy of Julie Mathis.

Though the mysterious patron has been named Malcolm, it is still not clear who he was in his past life. He revealed very little to the visiting psychic and may want to remain a mystery.

Our curiosity still not being satisfied, we decided to do more research. We found out that the lower wine cellar was a prison for Confederate soldiers during the Civil War. We could simply speculate that Malcolm was one of these prisoners or perhaps even a prison warden who has some unfinished business at the winery.

Or perhaps the mystery can be cleared up by a tragic love story that occurred about 138 years ago. Legend has it a "young German fellow" was discovered hanging from wooden rafters on the second floor following a failed love relationship. "The poor soul," it was said, "had immigrated to America in search of a dream." But his dream did not end on that day. He continues his quest with diligence and perseverance in days that seemingly have no end. And at night, Malcolm waits tirelessly at table 249, for the return of his lost love....

The Timeless Arcade

...a time to break down, and a time to build up;

—Ecclesiastes 3:3

At 7:33 P.M. on the evening of February 22, 2002, Lorain City firefighters were summoned to a blaze at the historic Duane Building at 387-401 Broadway in the heart of the downtown district. In spite of icy temperatures, which made fighting the fire more difficult, the sirens went screaming into the night, racing against time to salvage what was left of the historical edifice.

Listed in the National Register of Historic Places, the three-story structure was consumed by smoke and flames when the firefighters arrived. As far as they knew, the dilapidated building had been cleared of all occupants before their arrival. Moments later, a frightened spectator witnessed something startling from her position across the street: human images peering through third floor windows into the night.

"The night of the fire, I drove over to 4th St. and watched the scene of the fire from a parking lot across the street. I looked at the windows in the front of the building and on the third floor and I couldn't believe what I saw. It looked like firefighters standing in front of the windows. The flames were intense behind them. It seemed unlikely that they could be there but it looked like figures of men in the windows."

Her images left her with an unsettling feeling. No matter how much she tried to rationalize and come up with a logical explanation for those men standing in the windows of a burning building, she came up short. Yet one thing was certain, she did not doubt what she saw. She began to talk to others about what she saw. Then she came across a woman who offered perhaps the only possible explanation: the men in the burning building were spirits.

It is interesting to note that fire investigators determined that the fire was started on the third floor. Though they ruled out arson, they believed that it was started in one of the building's gas fireplaces by squatters trying to keep warm.

The Duane (Robinson) Building after the fire.

Lorain, Ohio, is located about 22 miles west of Cleveland at the mouth of the Black River on Lake Erie's Southern Shore. Originally known as "Black River Township" in 1807, it was re-named "Charleston" in 1833, and was officially incorporated as "Lorain" in 1873.

The city boasts of many famous sons and daughters, including Rear Admiral Ernest J. King, Supreme Allied Naval Commander in WWII, and Major General Quincy A. Gillmore of Fort Pulaski Fame during the American Civil War. It is also the birthplace of authors Toni Morrison, Helen Steiner Rice, Mark Nesbitt, and actor Don Novello, who preached over TV airwaves as Father Guido Sarducci on NBC's *Saturday Night Live*.

But the city's rise as an industrial power is what put it on the map. Lorain would eventually become a home base for United States Steel (est.1901), the Thew Automatic Shovel Company (est.1895), The American Shipbuilding Co.(est. 1899) and the Ford Motor Co.(est.1958). The city was clearly on the move.

When Architect Hamilton E. Ford began drafting plans for the Duane Building in 1901, he chose the Second Renaissance Revival Style to demonstrate the city's economic power. His sketch included an elaborate atrium and staircase adorned with towering ferns, and an exterior embellished with grooved sandstone pilasters and Roman-arched center windows.

The building became know as "The Arcade" because of its architectural style, unique shops, and amusement-park atmosphere. Citizens gathered at its storefront in a daily hustle-and-bustle of activities, which included catching an electric streetcar, shopping, or just lounging in the downstairs atrium.

But tragedy would batter the town when the "Lorain Tornado," still the worst in Ohio history, swept in off the lake on June 28, 1924, killing seventy-eight people and injuring a thousand more. Miraculously, the Duane Building escaped unscathed, unlike the State Theatre Building next door, where fifteen persons entered into their eternity.

Perhaps even more devastating was "The Great Depression" that knocked the town back on its heels in 1929, a blow from which it would never fully recover. Over the next five decades, many of the city's once mighty industries ceased operations or relocated to larger cities. Most downtown merchants were forced to close their doors. Of the few that remained, none had persevered quite like the spry lady florist who resided at the "Arcade," at 401 Broadway.

Born in the late 1800s to immigrant parents, Irene O'Malley and her family re-located to Lorain where she dreamed of becoming a florist. She began reading trade journals and attending floral shows, making it her life's work by the time she was twenty. After working in a downtown floral shop, she started her own business in the late 1930s. She operated her shop for the next twenty years until the economy forced her to move.

Irene moved her retail floral business in 1961 to apartment number one at the Duane Building, where she had resided for the 28 years since her husband's death. She took her last breaths there in 1965, ones that were sweetened by the scents that had adorned her apartment for so many years.

Not long after her passing, Lorain had been further reduced into a virtual ghost (no pun intended) town, with many of its structures, including the Duane Building, in an alarming state of decay. It was about this time that its residents began noticing unexplainable events throughout its rooms and halls that defied all reason.

"I heard stories that the lady who ran the upstairs flower shop in apartment number one passed away there, and that her spirit was still in the building," said one of the building's resident managers. "When I first moved in, the landlady told me I was welcome to use the ironing board in the old flower shop (now a utility room), but that I would have to get the key from her to unlock the door. I was a little nervous, but went down anyway."

She said she cautiously entered the room and shouted, "I'm not here to bother you, I just want to iron my clothes." Suddenly, the door slammed and she took off running, refusing to return for a long while.

Many residents complained about their toilets running when they were not actually flushed, believing that they were faulty. One went so far as to say that this flushing sound "followed her" even when she traveled. It was only after she spouted off the words, "Oh my God...it's following us again," that the sound desisted.

Other residents testified of smelling smoke and hearing voices at the bottom of the staircase where the Atrium used to be. "When you got to the first floor, you would smell pipe or cigar smoke," a resident stated. "I remember being told that people used to gather there back in the old days, after shopping or when waiting for a bus. A lot of times I could pick out a word or two, but could never make sense of what they were saying."

A couple was in their apartment in the Duane Building, talking about Mrs. Robinson, who had just passed a few weeks before. She was the millionaire owner of the Duane Building who allegedly was unwilling to update it. As they were talking, the phone rang and a woman asked for Mrs. Robinson. The witness swears that no one associated with Mrs. Robinson would have had that number. Sound like a coincidence? Not if you are the witness. The questionable events along with an overwhelming feeling are enough proof for any eyewitness of the paranormal.

And, even more bizarre (and just downright creepy), the apartment manager told of someone climbing into bed with her while her boyfriend was at work. "Shortly afterward, I would hear snoring sounds and could feel someone knocking the edge of the bed, as if they were getting up for a drink of water."

By the year 2000, the once elegant Duane Building had hit rock bottom, sinking like the Titanic to unknown depths, pulling the downtown area with it. Certain lost souls, who huddled around crude potbelly stoves in the vacant apartments, had become the building's only occupants, along with the resident vermin.

But the Millennium brought a fresh "Renaissance" Spirit to the city, one that was spearheaded by a new mayor and a high-profile developer. City parks and downtown buildings were given facelifts, and there were plans "to restore the Duane Building much as it was, with about nineteen apartments and two major storefronts." The project was to be completed by December 2003, that is, until the tragic winter fire of 2002.

The blaze was ruled accidental with no loss of life. Investigators determined the cause to be a faulty potbelly stove. And thanks to the swift response of the fire department, the structural walls remained intact, allowing for a continuum in the project timetable. But what about the human images witnessed in the third floor windows by the woman across the street?

She would later ask her husband, the Lorain Fire Chief, about them. He retorted, "there could be no way that anyone could have been in that building, the fire was too intense!" Little did the Fire Chief know that he had just proven his wife's theory.

The Duane Building has re-opened it doors and its sandstone pilasters are, metaphorically speaking, supporting the hopes and dreams of an entire town. There are new storefronts, new luxury apartments, and a set of fresh faces. In 2012, the building's restorers received an Award of Merit by Ohio's Historic Preservation office for the preservation and rehabilitation of the 1906 building. And, we're sure that there are times when the sweet smell of roses permeates the smoke-filled air, serving as a gentle reminder of glory days gone by.

Renovated Duane Building today.

The Curse Of The Painted Pony

"...for the city was doomed when it took in that horse, which brought death and destruction to the Trojans."

—Homer

There is one tourist attraction that puts the city of Sandusky, Ohio, on the proverbial map—a little amusement park called Cedar Point. Heard of it? Well, if you live within a hundred mile radius of Sandusky then you must have. It is arguably the country's greatest amusement park, boasting 16 roller coasters or "scream machines" as they so eloquently refer to them.

In the summer of 2013, the park is set to debut it's newest thrill ride "Gatekeeper." They claim it is the longest winged roller coaster on the planet, with the longest drop of any winged roller coaster. Normally a claim like this from any other amusement park would seem quite arrogant, however, anyone who has been to Cedar Point and experienced its *Demon Drop Magnum XL 200*, or *Millennium Force* would know to take their claims of fastest, longest, and/or scariest quite seriously. People travel great distances to experience the thrills of this popular amusement park.

Cedar Point is also very family oriented and features a variety of tamer things for kids to do which include *Soak City Waterpark*, pint-sized coasters and rides in *Snoopy Town,* and the horse carousel in *Frontier Town.* There was a time when the latter was not so benign. Many strange and startling occurrences have been attributed to a mysterious wooden horse referred to as the "Muller Horse" after its creator. It was reported that children often refused to mount the suspicious looking horse, fearing that they would be seriously injured. Even during peak summer months, employees reported the carousel running at less than full capacity.

But it was after closing time that the strangest things took place, as a former park employee explains in this frightening testimonial.

"The park is always closed when it happens. Many employees were living in an old hotel called the Cedars (circa 1903), and I moved there in 1989 when I became employed as a park historian. I would often drive around Perimeter Road to return home and pass the Frontier Town Carousel. Suddenly, it would start up with pipe organs blaring and hundreds of lights illuminating the nighttime sky. When the park employees finally arrived, they would always have a difficult time stopping it. There would be strings of burned-out bulbs that were always 13 in number."

Others claimed they had witnessed a mysterious woman near the "Muller Horse" as the carousel made its unscheduled revolutions. "After the carousel fired up," someone explained, "a ghostly woman appeared like a Banshee next to the hell-horse whose eyes would take-on a fiery, red glow as it galloped along its circuitous route."

Created by Daniel Muller for the William Dentzel Steam and Electric Carousel Company, the "Military Style Horse" had been sculpted in the classic, "Philadelphia Style" of woodcarving that stresses extreme realism. In 1921, it was placed on a carousel at Exhibition Park in Aurora, Illinois. The carousel was later moved to Lake Lansing Park, Michigan. Cedar Point purchased it in 1971, where it operated as the "Frontier Town Carousel" for twenty-three seasons. It was at Cedar Point that a number of ghostly legends evolved from the wooden horse that became known as "The Haunted Steed."

Mueller's Armored Horse from a sketch by Doug Dziama.

In 1994, the carousel was consigned to Dorney Park near Allentown, Pennsylvania. The controversial "Haunted Steed" and another Muller piece, "The Armored Horse," were removed for display at the Town Hall Museum. It is interesting to note that once relocated, the Dentzel Carousel ceased its strange nocturnal activity, although bizarre and frightening occurrences continued at Cedar Point.

Legend has it that attempts to photograph the horse may jam your camera or yield less than desirable results. "Either the head, legs, or some body part was missing…or it was distorted or blurry," explained a former park employee.

"I had been trying to photograph it for years and could never get a clear picture," said a local writer. "There were always hot spots, blurs, and other distortions. I even went out once at 8:00 A.M., only to unravel a totally blank film roll when I got home," she explained. "I returned a year-and-a-half later and the same thing happened."

Even more disturbing were the testimonials that those who attempted to capture the spectral steed on film were plagued by "bad luck."

It was April 2001. A local charter Captain was towing a paddlewheel boat along Lake Erie's southern shore. The waters were unusually calm for springtime. Sailing west toward Sandusky, his stomach knotted as he approached Avon Point, an area known for treacherous seas, sudden squalls, and shipwrecks. He turned around to check the tethered craft, only to make the chilling discovery that it had mysteriously vanished.

It is intriguing to note that the Charter Boat Captain had attempted to photograph both Muller horses one week prior to his paddlewheel's strange "disappearance." Even more enigmatic is the fact that in spite of intensive search and salvage efforts, the craft has never been located. It remains at some obscure and unknown location on Lake Erie's murky bottom in the treacherous waters off of Avon Point.

In late spring of 2003, my two daughters and I, avid ghost hunters all, journeyed to the renowned amusement park to witness this engineering marvel. But our main purpose for going was to locate the Town Hall Museum at the center of Frontier Town, where we were told we would find the infamous wooden horse.

The clerk directed us to the left corner where we spotted three carousel horses that were displayed on a small platform. Had we not recently viewed an exact replica at the Merry-Go-

Round Museum in downtown Sandusky, the horse's identity would not have been known, for it stood unassuming and unmarked.

In light of the Captain's story and our own bothersome superstitions, we left our cameras at home, choosing instead to supplant the horse's image in our minds.

It looked defiantly animate, as if it possessed a latent energy that struggled to escape. I looked deep into its eyes, and it seemed to look back, fixating on my every move. Its ears pointed ominously forward like horns, giving it a devilish demeanor. I had the distinct feeling that there was nowhere to hide.

Susan, my oldest daughter, was even more disturbed by the wooden animal. Her face had lost all expression. "It invokes fear when you see it. I knew exactly which of the three on display it was the moment I saw it, and I never want to see that horse again!" She later admitted that she had contemplated "heading for the hills" after our meeting with the horse.

Replica of Mueller's Military Horse at the Merry-Go-Round in Sandusky, Ohio.

We thought we might be overreacting, until we interviewed a former museum clerk. "The lights of the room were at the back," she explained. "When I turned them off at night I had to walk past the horse to exit the building, and it always felt a little creepy," she said in a quivering voice.

After seeing this unnerving wooden animal it was not hard to spot the irony that the most haunted element in this huge amusement park was a ride made for children. No wonder the little tykes were afraid to ride the thing, even in daylight.

We left the museum pondering some unanswered questions. Who was the mysterious female spirit and why had she chosen to haunt the Muller horse? What exactly was the curse that we were warned about?

Through some research we learned that many believe that there was a young Cedar Point employee who was desperately in love with a beautiful girl. They had planned a rendezvous by the Carousel long after the last soul had left the park. Unfortunately for the young man, his beloved was in a tragic accident and never showed up for their meeting. It is this girl's spirit who supposedly visits the horse still looking for her lost love.

We then probed into the life of Daniel Muller looking for answers.

We learned that the German-born woodcarver had immigrated to America in 1882 and settled in Sunnytown, Pennsylvania, near the site of the Dentzel Carousel Factory. He was betrothed to Elizabeth Muhe in 1895, a local innkeeper's daughter.[1]

Of course, as disturbing legend would have it, it is thought that Daniel Muller did the unthinkable in slaying his beloved wife and stuffing her lifeless remains inside the creepy horse. There is no clear motive to accompany the story, other than the pure speculation that Muller might have found her with another lover.

According to two former park employees, a large crack traverses one of Muller's horses from top to bottom, suggesting that it was carved from two blocks of wood, or perhaps sawed in half at a later time. During our visit, we had no trouble discerning the large fissure.

The Director of the Merry-Go-Round Museum told us that the only thing known about Mrs. Muller's life is that she died very young. It is interesting to note that the Dentzel Carousel was completed in 1921, which many people approximate as the time of Elizabeth's death.

Epilogue

A controversy exists as to which Muller horse is actually the legendary "Haunted Steed." The "Armored Horse," which was the object of a postage stamp issued in 1988, stands at center-stage next to his "Military Style Horse" which is at stage right. Cedar Point does not advertise the legend but acknowledges the "Military Style Horse" as being the one in question. Many former park employees, including the Charter Captain, disagree. We, of course, have our verdict in…do you?

Where Have All The Children Gone

> *"Are here all my children?"*
>
> —1 Samuel 16:11

The final eulogies were uttered as the snow began to fall. The old woman leaned over and adorned each of the four earthen mounds that covered the graves of her beloved grandchildren with a delicate red rose. She wiped the dirt from her hands as she made her way back to the house, breathing into them occasionally to keep warm. The winter of 1893 had been exceptionally brutal, but on this cold day in late January nature had delivered her cruelest blow.

Upon returning home from the gravesites, she put a large kettle of soup over the fire. She summoned her four grandchildren for supper. After dinner, she kissed them tenderly and tucked them into bed. The house became deathly quiet as she retired to the large front room having given herself up to her macabre mad nightly ritual.

The story of Gore Orphanage is quite possibly the textbook definition of an urban legend. Those of us who grew up in Northeast Ohio know the legend well by junior high school. In high school it is not uncommon to be triple dog-dared to go to Gore Orphanage Road at night and stay long enough to hear the cries of the unsettled souls of the children caused by the tragic ends of their young lives.

But what really happened on the infamous road? Much has been documented and speculated about the story of the alleged orphanage, which includes the evil schoolmaster dubbed "Old Man Gore" who had an insidious desire to murder small children to collect the insurance money. Even the name "Gore Orphanage Road" was spun from "Gore Road," its original name. Gore Road did not get this name from the alleged killings that took place on the winding road, but rather for a small piece of land that was annexed to the city of Lorain and just happened to resemble the gore of a dress—a triangular insert made of fabric that adds volume to the hem of a garment.

The legend of Gore Orphanage just may be the most famous in the area. Its story lines practically write themselves and have done so for the past 100+ years.

The tales became heightened during 1960s with an endless cast of characters. There was the hideous one-armed man, the "Headless Harley Rider," and "The Monster of Peasley Hollow," who stalked its prey by slinking from tree to tree—we know him today as "Bigfoot."

Numerous other phenomena were reported throughout the valley: blood-curdling screams, the smell of smoke, the crackle of roaring flames, and strange howling noises.

The story's origins seem to have been based on the "Light of Hope Orphanage" that stood on the bluffs overlooking Swift's Hollow, combined with the Collinwood School fire in 1908 that claimed the lives of 176 children. Although one of the orphanage buildings caught fire after its closure, it was the catastrophic burning of the Swift Mansion in 1923 that started all the folklore. In researching this legend, we have found that there are so many versions that it's hard to decipher the actual facts. It is reminiscent of the childhood game of "telephone" in which the person at the end of the chain receives a completely different version of the message than that which originated with the first person. It is very confusing, so in an effort to help clarify the origins of the story, we're going to go back to where we believe it all started.

Swift Mansion site where many believed the legendary "Gore Orphanage" stood, with example of Orb energy on the left side.

It stood about a half a mile south of the Gore Orphanage Bridge and is the site revered by hundreds of local teens. Built in the early 1840s by Joseph Swift, the fourteen-room Greek revival style mansion was very fashionable. It featured ornate marble pilasters and a vast ornamental garden.[1] Swift named his mansion "Rosedale" and lived there until an investment-gone-sour forced him to move. Following his departure from "Swift's Folly,"[2] as it was known by neighbors, it was rumored that Joseph Swift vanished from any known accountability in the mid-1860s.[3]

A farmer from New York named Nicholas Wilbur moved his family into Mr. Swift's unoccupied edifice. Listed as a solid citizen with strong political views, he chose Northern Ohio's fertile farmlands as the place to raise his family. He and his wife Eliza J. begot a son named Miller, who married

Hattie E. Kellogg and took up residence in nearby Berlin Heights, Ohio.

Miller and Hattie had three sons, including twin boys, and a daughter. At the beginning of the winter of 1892, the children ranged in ages from two-and-one-half to eleven-and-one-half years. The children's grandparents were particularly fond of them, nurturing them as if they were their own. The elderly Mrs. Wilbur developed a maternal-like love for them.

She especially looked forward to having them over the holidays and became extremely depressed when it was time for them to leave. To make matters worse, January 1893 brought frigid temperatures to Northern Ohio along with a widespread diphtheria outbreak. Described as a highly infectious illness, a deadly microbe called corynebacterium diphtheria enters through the mouth and nose. It attacks the mucous membranes, causing them to secrete a powerful toxin that damages the heart and central nervous system. It is a bold and contemptuous killer of children.

The January 18th edition of the Sandusky Daily Register told of a terrible tragedy to an area family: "It falls upon us to chronicle the saddest circumstance this week we have ever had to write for a paper, it being the sickness and death of two children of Mr. and Mrs. Miller Wilbur, the same being caused by that dreaded disease, diphtheria."

Ironically, as the news hit the presses, their two surviving siblings would be taken as well. It was in fact every parent's worst nightmare. In the course of only seven days four young lives would be wiped out. It was even more abominable than a murderer, because justice could never be served.

It proved too much for the family to bear. The January 25th edition of the Sandusky Daily Register would further chronicle the tragedy.

The Wilbur Children's Plot at Maple Grove Cemetery near Vermilion.

"The sympathy of our people can never be expressed in words to the grief stricken parents. Mr. and Mrs. (Miller) Wilbur are now in Birmingham, having been summoned to the bedside of Mr. Wilbur's mother, who is dangerously sick."

Although not terminal, it was said the illness altered her mind to a tormented and psychotic state. Little by little she lost touch with reality. Grandmother to the fallen children, Hattie Wilbur, eventually lost her wits and began "caring" for her grandchildren long after they were deceased. In the evenings, she would attempt to contact them using her "psychic" communications. Who could blame this grieving grandmother?

Witnesses say this pattern of behavior continued for six years, until her death on November 10, 1899. According to public record, Eliza J. Wilbur, aged 70 years and 6 months, died at her home from a valvular disease of the heart.

Fourteen months later, her beloved husband would reunite with her. After the house became vacant, travelers on Gore Orphanage Road were often enticed into its empty corridors by strange and seductive sounds that were emitted from within its walls. A fire in 1923 reduced the structure to a dark and silent shell, putting an end to all that was strange and paranormal...or did it?

In October 1993, a mother and her young son began experiencing strange phenomena at their residence along the Vermilion River near Wakeman, Ohio. For those unfamiliar with the area, the Vermilion River twists and turns as it flows through Wakeman, Birmingham, Swift's Hollow and Mill Hollow, before emptying into Lake Erie at Vermilion. Her son Andrew, age five, could not wait to play with his friend every day along the banks of the river. She proclaimed that he possessed the ability to forecast futuristic events, such as to when the drawbridge in Lorain, Ohio, would open next.

"My son would play near the edge of the woods and return home to tell me that his friend had a lot of 'neat' toys and things to play with. He told me his companion resided in a trailer in the woods, but knowing of no such residence, he became angry when I discredited him."

She asked him one more question. "What is your friend's name?"

His response was rather chilling. "Johnny Wilbur." He never mentioned the name again.

Although vandalism may have been the reason, it is likely that the fire was arson, perpetrated by someone wanting to mask the truth. Although most traces of physical evidence were destroyed, the alternate energy that rises from the dark hole that was once the mansion's foundation may someday shed some light on the strange and unsolved mysteries of Swift's Hollow.

Shine On Crescent Moon

...moreover the light of the moon shall be as the light of the sun
—Isaiah 26:30

No other celestial body has conjured more folklore than the moon. To early civilizations it was everything from a lucky symbol to an object of worship. And in spite of the fact that earthlings took "one small step" on it, it remains as enigmatic as ever.

If nothing has conjured up more folklore than the moon, it is arguable that no other island has conjured up more shenanigans than Lake Erie's own South Bass Island, also known as Put-in-Bay. For those of us from the area, Put-in-Bay's numerous bars, shops, and restaurants create an atmosphere that could be considered Lake Erie's island answer to Mardi Gras. The island is home to the Beer Barrel Saloon, which features the "World's Longest Bar," a 405 foot long bar, with 160 bar stools, 56 beer taps, and a seating capacity of 1200. When summer is in full swing, there is no place more happening than the Beer Barrel Saloon.

Though the Beer Barrel Saloon contains the "Longest Bar," the Crescent Tavern could quite possibly boast the title of "Most Haunted Bar." The Tavern's chief paranormal occupant is believed to be none other than TB Alexander, first mayor of Put-in-Bay, chief tourism promoter, and co-founder of the Put-in-Bay Yacht Club.

He was born Thomas B. (TB) Alexander on May 25, 1866, and his life was a most extraordinary one. In 1878, he began his acting career in Springfield, Ohio. He was discovered by the famous Maude Atkinson who made him her child protégé. Years later he starred as her leading man in such presentations as "Rupert of Hentzau" and "Graustark", becoming a matinee idol in his own right.

TB was also nicknamed "Dashing Tom" and was considered very handsome and charismatic. Thomas downplayed his rise to stardom and considered himself nothing more than an ordinary actor. When his company began touring, he became enamored with a lovely young pianist in his performing group named Edith M. Brown.

The daughter of John Brown, Jr., Edith was born in Put-in-Bay in 1866. Her father relocated there to become a surveyor and vineyard keeper, following his abolitionist father's execution in 1859. John Brown Senior was an advocate of the Civil Rights movement to abolish slavery. He believed that violence was the way to overthrow the institution of slavery. He famously led an unsuccessful attempt to capture the armory at Harpers Ferry, Virginia (now West Virginia), which led to his capture, conviction and eventual hanging.

Thomas and Edith were betrothed in her hometown on July 1, 1890, and retired there in 1908 when his acting career ended. The couple's golden years were more active than most, for it was here, and not on stage, that TB Alexander left his greatest legacy.

On June 20, 1908, TB and Edith purchased the Detroit House (originally the Hunker House Hotel) on Delaware Avenue. TB renamed the establishment the Crescent Hotel in 1910 and later expanded the building. That same year he was elected to a four-year term as village mayor. He was re-elected in 1919 and served until 1936, making him one of Ohio's most long-standing mayors. While in office, he also served as Justice of the Peace, Coroner, and President of Lake Erie Airways, helping him earn the title of "Island Father." He performed marriage ceremonies and helped with theatre productions at the local school. There is no doubt in our mind that South Bass Island was a charming place to live and had it's share of Hollywood glamour back in the day. In addition to TB Alexander, actress Ann Harding owned a cottage on the island. Ms. Harding was most famous for her Oscar nominated role of Linda Seton in *Holiday* (1930).

But sadly, near the end of his second term in 1935, TB's beloved Edith passed away. Coping the only way he knew how, TB turned to acting at nearby Port Clinton, where he directed and starred in a celebrated tale by Washington Irving. On March 17, 1936, about two weeks after the final curtain fell, Thomas B. Alexander would himself fall into a deep sleep, never to awaken. Being the romantic that he was, some speculate that he died of a broken heart.

The Crescent Hotel changed hands and was eventually transformed into a bingo hall and illicit slot machine parlor. The building lay abandoned for much of the 1970s, that is, until locals reported seeing strange blue lights illuminating the second floor and dark silhouettes peering from upstairs windows, giving the building a "lived-in" appearance.

The building reopened for business in the 1980s, following its acquisition by a prominent village merchant who dubbed it the Crescent Tavern. Paranormal activity increased, beginning with the appearance of an unidentified stranger in Hunker Hall, a dark and dreary upstairs corridor.

It was in a second-floor suite, now a business office, that TB and Edith made their summer home. Upon entry, one cannot help but notice a poster-size painting of man in a dark suit. His penetrating eyes, some say, can reach the depths of your very soul. It doesn't matter what part of the room you are in, you feel as if he is watching your every move.

Painting on the second floor of the former Crescent Tavern.

Next to the office is a small computer room. On a dark and gloomy night, it became the backdrop for this chilling testimonial as told by an employee working after hours.

"The room was abnormally quiet except for my tapping keyboard. Suddenly, the door squeaked open.... I could have sworn someone peered around the edge and peeked in, and then closed it back up again. At first I thought it was the manager, so I went downstairs hoping to find him, but the room was empty. I began searching the upstairs hall for an open window or something that could explain the strange phenomena."

Hunker Hall itself is a frightening place that many people choose to avoid. One employee said that it is a little creepy walking through it because the temperature can vary by as much as 30 degrees from end-to-end, even in 100-degree weather.

But the older gentleman in the dark, "turn-of-the-century suit" was not partial to Hunker Hall, for he had encounters with at least two persons at the downstairs level, as well.

The first was with a night maintenance man.

"I was mopping behind the bar after hours when I looked up and saw the full-length figure of a man dressed in early 1900's attire. I told him we were no longer open and that he would have to leave. When I turned around to escort him from the room…he was gone."

Another employee received a visit one evening from someone whose brazen entrance—and exit—went completely unnoticed.

"I had completely cleared the floor to give it a good sweeping. After about a thirty-second break where I peered out the window, I turned around to discover that one of the tray jacks had been set up in the middle of the room. I looked toward the adjacent taproom, but whoever was responsible was no longer there."

The locals decided that the spirit haunting Hunker Hall and the man in the portrait were one-in-the-same. But just who was he? One must examine the last days of TB Alexander for answers.

First, you may recall that TB traveled to Port Clinton, where he starred in a classic interpretation of Washington Irving's, *Rip Van Winkle*. Like his character, TB was awakened, but as a ghost, only to become a stranger in his own hometown.

More importantly, it was TB's wish that the community center and its local theatre be preserved for future generations. Not so coincidentally, a portrait of him in a dark, "turn-of-the century suit" was dedicated at the Town Hall Building on New Year's Eve 2003. It is interesting to note that December 31, 2003, marked the beginning of the first quarter crescent moon. Perhaps TB was promoting the arts as well as tourism from beyond the grave.

The Crescent Tavern circa 2003.

After the dedication ceremony in 2003, Hunker Hall was void of any paranormal activity. Many believe that TB returned to the grave to be with his beloved Edith. If true, it is possible he will slumber for another fifty years, or at least, until the next crescent moon appears over the enchanted island village of Put-in-Bay.

Epilogue

The Crescent Tavern was reopened as T&J's Smokehouse in 2012. It features numerous smoked items on its menu and a down home atmosphere where country music is as characteristic as the peanut shells that guests are encouraged to throw on the floor. T&J's is currently the only country bar/restaurant of its kind in Put-in-Bay.

The Spectral Handmaiden

The Soul is a Spiritual entity imprisoned in the body.

—Pythagoras

How would you respond If someone asked you to define the word "haunted"? Webster's Dictionary defines it as "supposedly frequented by ghosts." Sounds pretty simple, but what exactly does "supposedly" mean? And how about the word "ghosts," which suggests more than one? Is it possible that only one ghost can haunt a place?

The word "supposedly" is "something believed without sufficient proof" and a ghost is "the disembodied spirit of a dead person." Well that ought to clear things up.

Though we appreciate the iconic Dictionary's effort in defining the indefinable, one might still wonder, how often must ghostly visits occur and how many spirits are needed for a proper haunting?

The Gettysburg Battlefield in Pennsylvania is considered the most haunted place in America, and for good reason. Approximately 7,100 souls escaped from the decomposing bodies that contained them, with many remaining to search for closure to their once temporal existence. Their sheer numbers make this area a paranormal hotbed, where even novices can pretend to be experienced ghost hunters.

But what about the smaller places that are alleged to be haunted? Is it the place itself, or an actual spirit? Does the person from a previous life wish to stay under the spiritual radar? Evidence of a presence can be a sensory experience that could be as subtle as feeling that something or someone is there with you, even if that something cannot be seen. Things that are subtle to a person with psychic abilities may go undetected by others.

Located a block from Lake Erie in the "Old Plat" section of the original village of Huron, Captain Montague's Bed and Breakfast is a splendid Victorian-style home built circa 1820 by local lumberman John Wickham. In 1892 Wickham sold his majestic residence to Charles Z. Montague, a celebrated Great Lakes Captain.

Captain Montague's Bed and Breakfast.

Born in 1857, Charles was from the distinguished bloodline of Richard Montague who served as an advisor to President George

Washington. Captain Montague and his wife Sarah (Newton) moved into the stately mansion with their children Edith and Newton, and resided there more than thirty years.

But tragedy would eventually find them, starting with the untimely death of their beloved son Newton on September 6, 1901, at approximately 7 P.M. Newton Montague was just sixteen. At the time of his death he was a second year student at Kenyon Military Academy in Gambier, Ohio. He was ambitious and full of life. He had just returned from spending the summer with his father on the ship *Cornell* when he fell ill. Captain Montague was still at sea when his son passed and had to be reached via telegraph to return home for his son's funeral.

On May 11, 1923, twenty-two years later, the Captain himself perished aboard the ship, *John B. Cowie* during an ice-breaking mission near Whitefish Point, Michigan. The Captain was 66, and no doubt passed away living out his life's true passion. The elaborate Montague estate was sold after the death of Sarah Montague in 1939, at which time it became a business office and apartment house. Judy and Mike Tann acquired the property in 1994 and transformed it into a luxurious Bed-and-Breakfast.

The traveler today has numerous accommodation options to choose from: hotels, motels, condominium rentals and Bed-and-Breakfasts. Bed-and-Breakfasts (B&Bs) are known for their intimate hospitality and are often described as quaint, charming and "shabby chic" in décor. Some B&Bs are known for their family atmosphere, some for their character, while others, such as Captain Montague's former estate, are known for their subtle brand of paranormal activity.

The Tanns have been careful to preserve the Inn's Victorian décor to the finest detail, including the handcrafted front staircase, the ornate wooden floors, and many original wooden doors. There is an unmistakable Irish influence throughout, starting with the parlor that features a 1880s pump organ surrounded by spirited green walls and adorned with an extensive Irish Santa collection. They have won numerous awards including "Best in the Midwest" 2008-2009 by the "Best of Bed and Breakfast.com". The Tanns also host "Murder Mystery" weekends. We wonder if their permanent spiritual houseguests have ever actively participated in any of these mystery weekends.

Considering the building's long and colorful, yet tragic history, it would not seem unreasonable to assume the presence of a resident ghost or two. Judy denied ever seeing any uninvited houseguests during her ten years as innkeeper. But Judy did indicate that there were two women guests at two different times who felt a strong female presence near the back (west) staircase where the servants' quarters were located.

One of the women, a data manager from Butler County, Ohio, is a woman with an extraordinary sense of perception. Her husband, a firefighter, first discovered this after the couple started dating. He explained that she has an uncanny ability to sense things beyond normal human limits. He offered this chilling testimonial that almost defies logic.

"In 1972 there was a training manager at Station No. 7 in Hamilton, Ohio, named Stanley Meyer, who bore a striking resemblance to an aging John Belushi. He was often seen dressed in a smart blue uniform trimmed with gold buttons. One day, Stanley was called to assist with an industrial fire in nearby Oxford, Ohio, that threatened the building's very structure. Stanley lunged to push a fireman from a crumbling archway and lost his own life instead. Seventeen years later when my wife and I began dating, she came to tour Station No. 7 because it was allegedly haunted. After visiting the upstairs, she came down and told of an encounter with a man in a blue suit trimmed with smart gold buttons who had the bluest eyes she had ever seen, and a pointed nose that had a ball on the end. Her description matched a portrait of Stanley Meyer that hung somewhere in the building…one that she had never before laid eyes on."

After the coupled married, they went to Captain Montague's for a weekend getaway and stayed in the original Captain's

Quarters (which is now The Captain's Suite). The new bride offered an intriguing description of the house. "It is a really interesting place with abundant energy, but it is benevolent in nature. I could feel the presence of a young female, hard at work, making sure everything was in order. I could even feel her standing in the corner as we prepared for bed at night. It seemed to me as if she was second in command behind Judy [Tann]."

In 1999, they returned and stayed in The Dorothy Room where the Captain's servants resided. She experienced her most compelling feelings here, along with the stairway that ascended to it. "When we climbed the steps at night the hall light bulb would often be unscrewed, so it would not light, almost as if it were done intentionally. We would always screw it back in, but moments later it would be back out again. It became evident to me that the female spirit here was youthful and somewhat mischievous."

The couple returned once more in 2000. They stayed in The Edith Room (named for the Captain's daughter) near the front (east) of the home. There is a built-in bookcase in the room. "The books seemed to move by themselves, as if someone were arranging them in a particular order. One night I pushed a book back in that stuck out and the next day it was pulled back out again." But the woman noticed something wrong on this, their third visit. She had a feeling that something troubled the young servant girl or that she was not well. "I had this strange feeling that she was ill. She was in her early 20s and her name began with a 'M' like Millie or Millicent or Mildred. I'm not sure of the name, but I'm sure it began with the letter M."

Unfortunately, their weekend ended before an identity could be established. They couldn't help but wonder, who was the young girl and why did her estranged spirit return? What was her name?

Staircase where light bulbs are mysteriously unscrewed.

A census search for the year 1900 provided some answers. The residence at 229 Center Street listed five occupants: Charles Montague, head; Sarah Montague, wife; Newton B. Montague, son; Edith L Montague, daughter; *MAUDE WENTWORTH*, housekeeper.

Miss Wentworth was born in Ohio in 1880, making her 20 years old at the time of the census. She was single and listed as literate, with English being her primary language. A subsequent census search of 1910 records revealed that she had been replaced as the housekeeper for reasons that are unknown.

A search of local death records failed to turn-up her name. It is also possible that the youthful handmaiden was "swept off her feet" by a sailor who took her away from her laborious lifestyle, but if so, why had her spirit returned? If she was hoping to settle a grievance with her past employers, she might be out of luck, or is she? Maybe this story is a testament to our need to be comfortable with the unknown. Perhaps the answers lie only in the inner mind of someone with an extraordinary sense of perception, similar to that of the woman from Butler County, Ohio.

Depart All Ye Stranded Souls

*"And they begged him that he would not command them
to go out into the abyss"*

—Luke 8:31

It was the summer of 1925. The hot July sun appeared as a blazing ball in the western sky. The cool nighttime air would have to wait. To cope, the city's south-side residents fanned themselves with the evening newspaper and splashed on cold water. Many were immigrants who settled in Lorain, Ohio, to labor at the U.S. Steel Corporation's pipe and bar mills. Others fled the Iron Curtain in search of religious freedom, which could be found at numerous ethnic churches that dotted the South Lorain cityscape.

Near a tiny church on East 32nd Street, a youthful priest stared through his parlor window. The filtered sunlight outlined the face of a man that commanded instant respect, even away from the pulpit. Father Wasily had never been asked to perform such a task. His faith would be truly tested. Perspiration began dripping from his brow. He was relieved that there were three orthodox clergymen to assist him. As the sun made its final descent, the four men put on vestments, gathered holy water, and ignited incense. When they opened the door, they chanted in Church Slavonic (a language spoken in Eastern Europe) as they stepped out into the darkness. As the door closed behind them, a wide-eyed little girl of only seven bore witness from another room—what a sight it must have been in her young mind, one that was burned into her memory. After all, it isn't everyday that a posse of Holy men walked down the street singing, carrying bibles and incense burners.

Though we've all seen our share of exorcism movies (the godfather of them all being the 1973 classic *The Exorcist*) it is hard to imagine a person being possessed by demons and behaving like the unsuspecting little girl in the movie. There are also the so-called "based on true stories" movies like 2005's *The Exorcism of Emily Rose*, which seemed especially farfetched. We are highly suspicious of Hollywood's take on anything—though entertaining, these types of movies are most likely loosely based on a true story at best. Maybe the idea of a person being the devil incarnate in real life is farfetched. Or is it? The Christian Gospels cite numerous exorcisms in persons who today would be considered criminally insane. Many symptoms documented are similar from one to another, including extreme animation and disorientation along with a tendency toward destructive or violent behavior.

And let's not forget about the real life haunting of houses or other such buildings.

> *Imagine moving into your dream home. You've carefully selected the layout, which includes your desired number of bedrooms and baths, a spacious dream kitchen, and a cozy and functional family/living room. Perhaps there is even a fireplace with a chimney to warm you on a cold winter's night. Picture yourself happy, settled, and relaxed with your feet up sipping wine by the crackling fire. All is calm and peaceful. That is, until you suddenly hear the upstairs doors violently slam and footsteps pounding the floors. Maybe there is even a chill that*

enters the room (and your heart) that makes you shiver despite being by a fire; and the most unsettling part, some moaning or some other sound that you know is just not human. You hope that it's just a figment of an over-active imagination. But it happens again…and again. You want to run for the hills. When all hope is lost, you begin to wonder, can modern Christian clerics really exorcise spirits like Jesus and the Apostles did? Perhaps your next call should be to a clergyman.

Although no one knows for certain if demons can possess a human being or an inanimate object like a house, it is interesting to note that exorcism rituals are practiced to this day by certain Apostolic Christian Religions, particularly those in the Eastern Rite. This includes Eastern Orthodoxy, which is perhaps the most misunderstood Christian Church. Although historians mark the year 1054 AD as its beginning, many Orthodox faithful insist their church originated in 33 AD, the year they believe Jesus arose from the dead and ascended into Heaven. The church has gained notoriety for its "weeping" icons and its Easter observance, which believers say must occur on the first Sunday after the full moon after the Jewish Passover. All of this has contributed to the church's mystique.

Father Wasily had heard strange tales as a seminarian from the mountain folk, but at this moment, it was a young couple's desperate pleas that haunted him. Though they were not religious, they had nowhere else to turn. Shortly after moving into the two-story home on East 29th street in Lorain, they began hearing bizarre noises from an upstairs bedroom.

"We dreaded going to bed at night. The hideous sound reverberated from the vacant bedroom above: thump—slide, thump—slide, thump—slide. My husband would go upstairs only to find an empty room. When he returned to bed, it continued all over again: thump—slide, thump—slide, thump—slide. We became sleep deprived. After a while, we had even hoped to find an intruder, whose presence, however threatening, would have at least offered closure."

After ceremoniously trekking the three long blocks, the four clergymen arrived at what they believed was an empty home. Father Wasily requested the couple stay away during the ritual, not wanting them to witness anything disturbing.

Father Wasily recalled: "We felt an undeniable presence when we entered the home. We stopped at every corner and offered relentless prayers and holy water. We felt a resistance as we moved from room to room. When we ascended the stairway we could feel the force weaken somewhat. After repeating the ritual upstairs, we entered the bedroom where we implored the spirit to leave. Suddenly, as if in a violent windstorm, the curtains over an open window were sucked outside in a loud 'swoosh' that left a deafening stillness."

Father Wasily (front and center) with priests from the Midwest Diocese. Photo courtesy the Dziama family.

After hearing this incredible story as retold by Father Wasily's daughter, who was seven at the time, we began thinking of ways to validate something that sounded so much like a Hollywood script. We consulted a Russian Orthodox archpriest who was not surprised by this testimonial. He, too, believes that "there is another dimension out there."

"I have served at Saints Peter & Paul Church many times. Late one evening, I peered from the altar to witness a woman in white kneeling in prayer. It is not unusual for persons to enter the church after hours, but the strange thing was I did not hear her come in. I turned back toward what I was doing, only to discover that she was gone when I was finished, and, just like before, I did not hear her leave."

He explained that this was not an isolated incident and that people are often heard coughing when the church is empty. He went on to say that he had experienced a persistent spirit while at a mountain cabin in Pennsylvania's Laurel Highlands, near the tiny village of Black Lick.

"I was asked to bless the home of a recluse by his young godson. It was a bitterly cold January day. We had to literally climb on all fours to reach the summit. When I entered the one room dwelling, there was a little old man there. I had an eerie feeling about the place from the start. I began anointing the room with holy water while chanting petitions for cleansing and purification. All of a sudden, some wooden chairs slid violently across the floor as if they were kicked or shoved! The young man stood in awe as I walked over to bless a mirror. When I was finished, a large crack developed over the pane that formed the shape of a cross. The young man looked at me and said, 'Father, I think we did our job.'"

A few weeks later, he called the archpriest to tell him his godfather had passed away. In what seems as an ironic twist of fate, the old man's spirit appears to have waited for that redeeming day in January, one that served as its final vindication.

This strange story led me to inquire about clergymen dismissing unclean spirits from people. The archpriest told me of an experience he had had in a hospital mental ward that, in my opinion, offers a stunning testimonial to a modern human exorcism.

"I was walking down the hallway wearing a clerical collar when a patient shouted out at me 'Hey, you Son of a B _ _ _ _,' drawing me to the bedside of a contemptible old man."

"Are you talking to me?" I said.

"Hey, you know what? You're a smart Son of a B _ _ _ _ _, aren't you? How come you're not afraid of me?" he demanded.

"Well, since you're the one hooked-up to iv's and I'm the one wearing tennis shoes, I at least figured that I could run faster than you!"

"As the man settled down, I sat by his side and he confessed that he had been abusive to everyone around him, including his family. I began praying with him and crying with him, and ended up staying most of the night. He asked for forgiveness. I said I could not grant that but would make a petition for him. I learned that he had passed away peacefully later that morning. I was saddened at his funeral when I was the only one there."

Not long ago, while he was at Saints Peter & Paul Church, the archpriest was approached by a professional photographer who requested permission to photograph the Church's interior for a magazine spread. After recording numerous exposures, the man left seemingly content with his work. A week later, he returned to show the archpriest the many white blemishes and unexplainable blurs that had utterly ruined his images.

SS. Peter & Paul Orthodox Church in Lorain.

"There is nothing wrong with your photographs," said the archpriest.

"Then how do you explain these erratic distortions?" the man challenged.

"That, my friend, is the way it is here!"

The man left defeated and bewildered. As the archpriest made his way back toward the altar, he smiled softly. "Those, my friend, are our many departed brothers and sisters, who have found their way home."

Epilogue

The archpriest continues to serve as pastor of a Cleveland area parish.

Father Wasily passed away on April 7, 1968 at the age of 72.

The 29th street home to which the four clergymen were called has been documented to be where an elderly woman died. We were told that when she walked she dragged one leg, the result of a stroke. Was her restless spirit the source of the "thump—slide, thump—slide, thump—slide?"

Lake Erie Monster: Creature Or Myth

Warning: The waters of Lake Erie are dangerous and unpredictable. Swim at your own risk.

—City of Huron, Ohio

Though the Lake Erie Coast is far from Hollywood in proximity (2,022 miles from Mann's Chinese Theatre on Hollywood Boulevard to be exact), we are not too far off in movie spirit (if you'll pardon our pun). Most people have seen Steven Spielberg's iconic horror classic *Jaws* (1975) and would probably be willing to admit that while taking a swim in the ocean they can't help but think of the blood-thirsty killer great white shark. The possibility of the events of *Jaws* taking place in real life is not beyond the scope of the imagination. If the possibility of a killer great white existing in salt water is real, then why wouldn't it be possible for a man-hungry creature to exist in the fresh waters of Lake Erie as well?

Every summer after school ended our family would take a vacation, which almost always included a visit to the ocean. After seeing the movie *Jaws*, we felt it necessary to institute an ocean game to quell our nerves upon entering the salty waters. The rules of the game were quite simple–when swimming in the ocean, you must never be the furthest one out. In other words, always make sure you are behind someone while in the water for if the unlikely event of a shark attack exists, you will have a head start to the shore! Little did we know that fear existed so close to home.

The town of Port Dover, Ontario, on Canada's southern shore, features a bustling Lake Erie harbor for commercial and recreational boaters. The inlet hosts the world's largest fresh water fishing fleet, where yellow perch and pickerel (walleye) are harvested. The town marina near the Coast Guard Station provides small boat launching facilities, while the yacht club at Black Creek offers guest slips for pleasure craft. The area is best known for "Friday the 13th," an annual event for motorcycle enthusiasts.

But the town was rocked in July 2001. Three swimmers were attacked on a beach near the Port Dover Pump House by an unknown aquatic creature. The first victim was a woman who was bitten on the right calf while paddling near shore. The following morning, a man and a child suffered painful bites while swimming in the same waters.

The emergency room physician indicated the woman had circular jaw-like puncture marks some six inches apart, suggesting an enormous mouth. After ruling out gobies, lamprey eels, snapping turtles, walleye and muskellunge, he stated "the wounds were not consistent with any animal I have ever seen."

The word "cryptozoology" is derived from the Greek words kryptos (hidden), zoon (animal) and logia (study). Unlike science, it is based on conjecture rather than proof, and has been quick to accept some of Nature's darkest mysteries. It is in this classification one must place the attacks.

Science closed the book on the Port Dover incident, allowing in essence, a creature of extraordinary proportions to be at-large in Lake Erie's open waters. Many suggested the savage attacks could only have been made by Bessie, Lake Erie's legendary sea monster.

With sightings as far back as the 17th Century, Bessie has been described as a grayish serpentine beast measuring from

30 to 40 feet in length. Many early reports originated from Canadian shores and described it as something coiled, snake-like and fearsome-looking.[1] Unfortunately, along with the spread of the monster hype came the hoaxes and practical jokes.

Perhaps the most famous spoof was the "capture" of a large serpent by two Cincinnati anglers in 1931. While fishing in Sandusky Bay, they clubbed the reptile and placed it in a wooden crate. A local biologist identified the specimen as an adult Indian Python. The two fishermen, members of a touring carnival, were long gone when the story hit the headlines.[2]

In the early 1990s, a flurry of sightings by recreational boaters, charter captains, and shoreline observers near Huron, Ohio, occurred in numbers too large to ignore. A local marina owner offered a bounty for a live capture, a scientist was consulted for identification purposes, and the city's mayor declared Huron the "National Live Capture and Control Center for the Lake Erie Monster."

Critics held the city in ridicule, but even though the sightings occurred at different times and in different areas over a span of 20 years, the chronicles were all very similar. A home video taken at Kelleys Island in 1993 brought the alleged creature into our living rooms.

Those who claim to have seen the creature have offered similar descriptions: "it lumbered beneath the surface with a deliberate, undulating motion, and was between twenty to thirty feet in length. The body shimmered as it broke water, suggesting a shiny or scaly, reptilian-like outer skin."

A boater captured pictures while photographing a sunset at the marina just east of town. A local maritime museum director concluded that the camera position was too far away for a positive identification. We would have to agree. But like the Port Dover incident, experts did not take the video very seriously.

We interviewed two Huron area residents who reported sightings in 1990 that resembled the Kelleys Island images.

Although the stories did not provide conclusive proof, the similarities were chilling. The first came from a local marina owner.

"I was fishing with my sister just east of the Huron Lighthouse when she noticed a strong wave action nearby. I looked beyond the bow and witnessed an up-and-down churning motion with the sun shining on it."

He said that a local charter boat captain saw a similar object northeast of the Huron Lighthouse later that summer. With a capacity crew on board, he followed the anomaly until it disappeared into the depths.

Huron Lighthouse at Nickle Place Beach.

The second testimonial came from a fire inspector who was touring an apartment building about a mile west of town in September 1990.

"The wind came from the Southwest on a calm and sunny day. The time was about 3:30 P.M. At that moment, I looked toward the Northwest and an object appeared about twenty-five yards from shore. What I saw was big: about twenty to thirty feet long, dark gray, with armor-plated skin. It appeared in two groups, and I could not discern a head or tail. Although it seemed to not be moving, it was gone when I returned a minute or two later. I'd never seen anything like it."

Science, by-and-large, has justified strange phenomena such as these with theories that fail to disprove them. For example, there is the "floating log" and "submerged rock" theories, which might apply to some sightings. Driftwood is most common in spring after the winter ice melts, but occasionally occurs after powerful summer storms. The stories from this writing took place between June and October in benevolent weather. As for submerged rocks, had the charter captain been "following" them, he would have most certainly run aground.

Then, there is the "estuary" theory, which is a connecting water passage between an inland stream and an ocean or lake. Fish may become "trapped" inside them following water level fluctuations or wind-induced sand barriers, and will collectively "dash" toward open water once the obstruction is cleared. Some scientists believe it is this event that is actually witnessed in monster reports.

Although estuary habitats exist at Old Woman Creek near Huron and North Pond on Kelleys Island, many creature sightings have been reported over open water, miles from shore. Biologists admit it is the Freshwater Carp, a shallow water scavenger that most often forages in estuaries, casting doubt over the theory's relevance to deep water. Furthermore, gulls, which are often present where fish are tightly schooled at the surface, were notoriously absent from these stories.

Therefore, if it is even remotely possible that a monster could exist in Lake Erie, how did it get there? Here are two theories that may provide answers.

The present formation of the Great Lakes dates to the late glacial period that began 32,000 year ago. Glaciers a mile thick advanced across Ohio to Cincinnati, melted, crumbled, and retreated back north. This cycle repeated again and again, carving depressions that eventually formed the world's greatest fresh water system. When the Ice Age ended around 7,000 years ago, fossilized remains of whales were discovered in the region, leading scientists to believe that an "appendage" from the Atlantic entered Lake Ontario via the St Lawrence Valley around 11,000 years ago. Although some Oceanographers believe a monster could have entered this way, they quickly point out it fails to prove its existence.

Shell Cove Park in Sheffield Lake where fossilized remains of a giant prehistoric fish were discovered.

The second theory involves the introduction of alien fish through bilge pumping by foreign ships. In recent years, marine species like Lampreys and Zebra Mussels have invaded this delicate fresh water ecosystem with near catastrophic results. It is estimated that a new species is identified about every seven months, faster than biologists can study them.

The Lake Erie Monster is but one of many mysteries surrounding this spectacular "Inland Sea." Of the 2,000 known shipwrecks here, only 265 have been documented. The most puzzling was the disappearance of the *Marquette & Bessemer No.2* on December 8, 1909. Bound for Port Stanley, Ontario, from Conneaut, Ohio, the passenger ship sank in a violent storm with 31 persons on board and a fortune of $50,000. There were no known survivors. The body of the First Mate, preserved in ice, washed ashore four months later near Niagara Falls. Ten months later, the Captain's remains were found near Long Point Beach Ontario. The wreck and the money have never been located.

We would be lying if we said we would not be a bit nervous while entering the waters of our beloved Great Lake after hearing all of the stories about the alleged unidentifiable creature. While swimming in the lake's waters we will try to keep a cool head and remain calm if something brushes up against us, or if we see any unusual wave action while heading to shore. After all it is probably just a tightly schooled group of fish…isn't it?

Stars And Stripes By The Bay

*"If it ain't Dixie, it don't feel quite like home.
My Southern Blood runs deep and true…."*

—John Jarrard/Kent Robbins

It was a frigid, fall day on Johnson's Island in the early 1900s. The youthful Lieutenant stared across Lake Erie's stormy waters as he thought about his home in Cherokee County, Alabama. He had been awakened by an enormous squall that produced gale-force winds, freezing rain, and deafening thunder. He thought about seeking shelter below the barracks, but chose instead to remain, staring in awe at the magnificent and oncoming tempest.

Growing up on the North Coast of Lake Erie, we have come to respect its raw might and power. Her shallow waters make it the most violent and unpredictable of the Great Lakes, enabling her to produce squalls and fierce winds in excess of 75 mph with little or no warning. Its murky floor is littered with the debris of 2000 documented shipwrecks, along with treasure from 265 of those that have not be found (referred to thereafter as "Ghost

Ships"). Her depths are a graveyard of human remains, their identities known only to God.

Sandusky Bay is a land-locked body of water, approximately fourteen miles from east to west, with a north-south distance of about three miles. It averages only twelve feet in depth and receives water from the numerous tributaries that empty into it, including the Sandusky River. It is separated from Lake Erie by the Marblehead Lighthouse and Cedar Point Amusement Park to the east, and is divided- in- two by the three-mile-long Thomas Edison Memorial Bridge that connects Ottawa and Erie Counties. During shipping season, huge lake freighters depart from and arrive at Port Sandusky. To get to open water, which is about two and one half miles north of Sandusky, they have to pass Johnson's Island in the middle of nowhere....

Johnson's Island has little or no notoriety compared to Lake Erie's well known island resorts which have become popular tourist attractions, second only to Cedar Point Amusement Park. Put-in-Bay on South Bass Island, for example, has been dubbed the "Key West of the North," and for good reason. There you will find the "Long Bar," partying-in-the-park, local wineries, sidewalk minstrels, and the smell of barbeque chicken. A little to the east lies Kelleys Island, the largest island, known for the world famous Glacial Grooves, migrating butterflies, charming Bed-and-Breakfasts, and a serene island lifestyle. Closer to the mainland, one can discover Catawba Island near Port Clinton, Ohio, and its vineyards, marinas, vacation homes and restaurants.

Island ferry services included the dependable Miller Boat Line, the Kelleys Island Ferry, and the popular Jet Express, a high-powered pontoon boat boasting the "fastest way to Put-in-Bay." And don't forget the Goodtime I, where you can cruise to Kelleys and Put-in-Bay all in the same day, while enjoying waterfront dining, cocktails, and entertainment.

Johnson's Island, by contrast, can be reached from Bay Shore Drive on the Marblehead Peninsula via a half-mile causeway. There is an automatic gate that will lift after two one dollar bills are deposited into a small kiosk. There is no ferry service, but if a water landing is desired, one could choose to arrive by powerboat, kayak, or jet-ski.

The island was named for Leonard B. Johnson, who purchased the land for farming. It offered shelter from Erie's rough, open waters, and an extended autumn growing season. The soil was fertile and there was adequate irrigation. It was forested with hickory and oak, providing lumber for construction and fuel. In addition, there was a rock quarry that would increase the island's value.

Eventually, Leonard Johnson would end up leasing half his island during the Civil War. The United States Government established a stockade and barracks for holding Confederate prisoners of war. After functioning for about five years, the base ceased all military operations, with buildings and equipment being auctioned off or torn down. Years later, the Federal Government assumed control of the former stockade and adjacent cemetery. Today it is a National Historic Site funded and maintained by the United States Department of the Interior.

Cedar Point attempted to develop the private land into a resort after Mr. Johnson's passing, but without much success. The island returned to farming and began mining a nearby rock quarry, providing job opportunities for citizens and immigrant workers. Many came from as far away as Germany and Italy. It was at this rebuilding time that Italian quarrymen and construction workers arrived at Johnson's Island.

The quarry was on the other side of the island, away from the notorious and now historic prison site. The Italians began the arduous task of swinging sledgehammers and picks to break through the solid rock. Residents near the quarry and those passing by were "treated" to festive Italian songs, and could hear the men laughing, conversing, and telling stories, all in Italian. It appeared that they were not fluent in English.

Through the pounding of hammers and picks persons near the quarry heard strange sounds. The men were singing the spirited Southern hymn, "Dixie" in perfect unison, with each and every word enunciated in English. How and where could they have learned such a song? Why did they choose one associated with the American South? Had they selected "The Star Spangled Banner," there would have been little or no controversy.

New home construction began near the old fortification and on the island in general. During a fierce fall storm, workers heard bugles blowing and shouting reverberating from the cemetery. They witnessed soldiers dressed in a brownish-yellow or "butternut" colored uniform, marching in double-time, appearing to "rise up" from the graves. Frozen with fear, they tried to convince themselves they had witnessed a re-enactment, or possibly a local militia conducting a drill. None of them stayed long enough to find out, as they quickly fled to the mainland. When island residents were told the tale, many speculated they had been drinking, and quickly dismissed the incident.

Confederate Sentinel's silent vigil.
Some say, he breaks his silence at midnight.

Visitors to Johnson's Island can view the modest gated cemetery where 206 prisoners of war perished and are interred. Hand-carved wooden markers originally stood on the gravesites, but deteriorated due to harsh winds, rain, and snow. In 1890, good citizens from the State of Georgia replaced the aging markers with new marble ones. They are guarded by a bronze Confederate sentry, facing eternally southward, dedicated in 1910. Chapter 445 of The United Daughters of the Confederacy maintained the graveyard until it was acquired by the United States Government in 1932.

No longer are military exercises conducted there, and yet, some still observe soldiers marching and singing near the now defunct garrison. Others have witnessed the bronze soldier repositioning himself at midnight from his marble pedestal. All of this defies explanation and raises the question, who are the phantom soldiers that frighten residents and visitors alike around the island? The answer may lie in the graves of the 206 soldiers interred there.

Referred to as "Southern Pride," it is a cultural attitude common to the states below the Mason-Dixon Line. Ask any resident of Alabama, Georgia, or Tennessee, and you will receive the same response. It's about saying, "Please and Thank-You," and opening doors for ladies. It is about hard work, not working on Sundays, and giving thanks at the dinner table. It is an honest handshake among gentlemen, Grandma's home-made apple pie, and the warmth of a crackling fire. It is, in short, about living a simple, contented lifestyle.

And, if you should ask them where Heaven is, you will probably hear that it is "somewhere in Dixie." By now, it is our hope and belief that most, if not all, of the 206 souls who were buried on Johnson's Island have reached their heavenly resting place. But it is also our belief that some have not yet made it home.

Confederate cemetery. Some markers are simply "UNKNOWN."

It would not surprise us to hear the Italian quarrymen sing a different tune today. "If it ain't Dixie (it won't do)" by John Jarrard and Kent Robbins, would do well to explain the mysterious unrest that continues to haunt Johnson's Island:

> *"But now my wheels, they're rollin' southward*
> *And Heaven's comin' into view, oh yeah*
> *Home sweet home is Alabama*
> *That's what I look forward to.*

Endnotes

Death On The Pacific Express
1. Thomas Corts, ed., *Bliss and Tragedy. The Ashtabula Railway-Bridge Accident of 1876 and the Loss of P .P. Bliss.* (Sherman Oak Books, Samford University Press, 2003), 57. Bliss, a well-known gospel composer and wife Lucy were passengers on the doomed Pacific Express No. 5. His composition "Lora Vale" is a moving piece about a young girl's final moments here on earth.

The Perpetual Spirit
1. Clague Park is located about 10 miles west of downtown Cleveland, at the intersection of Clague and Hilliard Roads. It is beautifully landscaped, complete with ball fields, a swimming pool, picnic areas and a large duck pond. The Clague Playhouse is located behind the Clague Museum (Walter's home) at 1371 Clague Road.

The Cryptic Fort
1. Larry Nelson, *Men of Patriotism, Courage, & Enterprise! Fort Meigs in the War of 1812*, (Canton, Ohio: Daring Books, 1985), 132-133.
2. Nelson, *Men of Patriotism*, 117.

3. Freeman Cleaves, *Old Tippecanoe, William Henry Harrison and His Time*, (Charles Scribner's Sons, 1939, renewed by Freeman Cleaves, 1967), 171.
4. Alfred M. Lorrain, *The Helm, The Sword, and The Cross: A Life Narrative*, (Cincinnati: Poe & Hitchcock, 1862), 106, 145-146.
5. Nelson, *Men of Patriotism*, 54.
6. Nelson, *Men of Patriotism*, 81-82.

The Curse of the Painted Pony
1. Charlotte Dinger, *Art of the Carousel*, (Carousel Art, Inc., 1983).

Where Have All The Children Gone
1. Bill Ellis and American Folklore Society, *What Really Happened at Gore Orphanage?*, (Bill Ellis,1983), 4.
2. Ellis, *What Really Happened at Gore Orphanage?*, 4.
3. "Undiscovered Ohio—Economy Vacationland," by *The Western Reserve Magazine* (Garrettsville, Ohio: Thelma Bruce, 1976, 1978), 148.

Lake Erie Monster: Creature Or Myth
1. Loren Coleman and Jerome Clark, *Cryptozoology A to Z. The Encyclopedia of Loch Monsters, Sasquatch, Chupacabras, and Other Authentic Mysteries of Nature.* (New York: Touchstone, 1999) 36.
2. Coleman and Clark, *Cryptozoology*, 37.

About The Authors

Doug Dziama is a life-long Ohio resident. He graduated from Bowling Green State University with a degree in Radio and TV Broadcasting and a minor in Journalism. His stories have appeared in *Over the Back Fence Magazine* and *Paranormal Pennsylvania and Beyond Magazine*.

Doug and his wife Karlene have enjoyed over three decades of marriage. They have two daughters, Susan and Jennifer, and three grandchildren, Sahana, Charlie, and Megan. In his spare time Doug enjoys reading, vacationing, listing to music, entertaining by his backyard pool, and, of course, writing.

Jennifer Dziama Teed grew up on Ohio's North Coast. She is a graduate of the University of Detroit Mercy. Jennifer and her writing partner, teacher, friend, and father, Doug Dziama, share the desire to explore the history and ghosts of Ohio's North Coast. They also share a die-hard and tough love for their hometown "Tribe," the Cleveland Indians.

Jennifer and her soul mate and husband Joe live in Plymouth, Michigan. They have two children, Charlie and Megan. Jennifer is an avid movie-goer and writes reviews for cinemanerdz.com. Her first movie, *Chronic*, which she wrote and directed, is due to be released independently in the fall of 2013.

www.ingramcontent.com/pod-product-compliance
Lightning Source LLC
Chambersburg PA
CBHW071307040426
42444CB00009B/1910